19 WAYS TO SURVIVE: SMALL-BUSINESS STRATEGIES FOR A TOUGH ECONOMY

Lynn Spry and Philip Spry

Self-Counsel Press
(a division of)
International Self-Counsel Press Ltd.
USA   Canada

Self-Counsel Press acknowledges the financial support of the Government of Canada through the Book Publishing Industry Development Program (BPIDP) for our publishing activities.

Printed in Canada.

First edition: 2010

Library and Archives Canada Cataloguing in Publication

Spry, Lynn, 1974-

    19 ways to survive : small-business strategies for a tough economy / Lynn and Philip Spry.

ISBN 978-1-55180-891-8

    1. Small business--Management.

I. Spry, Philip II. Title. III. Title: Nineteen ways to survive.

HD62.7.S67 2010   658.02'2   C2010-900655-0

FSC

Mixed Sources

Product group from well-managed
forests and other controlled sources

Cert no. SW-COC-002358
www.fsc.org
© 1996 Forest Stewardship Council

Self-Counsel Press
(a division of)
International Self-Counsel Press Ltd.

1704 North State Street   1481 Charlotte Road
Bellingham, WA 98225   North Vancouver, BC V7J 1H1
USA   Canada

CONTENTS

TABLES

SAMPLES

To Our Children

NOTICE TO READERS

INTRODUCTION

A storm is looming on the horizon, the clouds are an angry gray, and the rough water is tossing the ship around like an eggshell. The ship's captain could turn back and wait for clear waters and mild winds, but that would mean losing the investment in this voyage, not to mention the lavish rewards for completing a successful trip. So the intrepid captain chooses to press on and weather the storm.

An equivalent to this brave and audacious captain is the entrepreneur who takes on the challenge of running a small business. The obstacles are large, but the rewards are even larger. A successful small business can propel the owner to financial freedom very quickly. Through franchises, taking the business public, or simply adding more stores, small-business owners have the chance to succeed in ways that most people working a nine-to-five job will never see. Owning a business is risky but the rewards are significantly greater. If it's done right, business ownership is the opportunity to make more money than any job can ever pay.

In these tough economic times, with unpredictable gas prices, a depressed real-estate market, and rising employee costs, the minor problems your business has had can be magnified many times. You may have already started to see the impact on your business. Maybe your sales have slowed, customer traffic has dwindled, or when customers do come in, they don't spend as much money. Your products and employees are becoming more expensive. Even if your business has been running successfully for years, it can be impacted. This isn't an isolated problem and you are not alone.

Some people will choose to shut down their businesses while others will sell and hope they make enough money to retire. Those worse off may simply close their doors and walk away, ignoring their debts and obligations. However, some people will face the challenges head on and, like the successful ship captain, they will prepare for the storm and ride it out. They will redesign their businesses to become successful during this tough economy. These redesigned companies will be well positioned to grow once the crisis is over.

You may be wondering how a small business can grow during this difficult time. It may be challenging, but it can be done. After all, many large companies were in this exact position at one time or another. This book was inspired by the challenges our own small business faced. In early 2006, in Arizona, at the height of the real estate boom, we purchased a small computer store: Arizona Computer Outlets. At that time, houses were selling for 30 to 40 percent more than the purchase price; within two or three days of being listed, sometimes within hours. The store was thriving in a market in which home equity loans were inexpensive and people had more cash than they could spend. Within a few months, the environment changed dramatically.

As interest rates increased, the Phoenix housing market began to tumble. Consumers who had adjustable rate mortgages on their homes saw their monthly mortgage payments rise dramatically. Their disposable income shrank as a larger percentage went to paying for their houses. As if that weren't bad enough, higher gas prices restricted consumer spending even further. By December 2006, sales in all industries were slowing and as a small local retailer, we felt the pressure of a slow holiday season.

Over the next seven months, store sales continued to slow, until we hit rock bottom in July 2007. The store lost more than $9,000 that month alone. We knew we needed to make significant changes, but had very few

solid ideas on what to do. We found that many books discussed opening a new store, but there were few resources targeted at turning around a small business. We knew that to stay afloat, we needed to change. Desperate to survive, we contacted other small-business owners, read all the business and management books we could find and, by September, had the start of a plan to recover our business.

Within six short months the business had turned around, even though oil prices had reached new highs and home prices had fallen more than 10 percent. Pundits around the country were starting to discuss the possibilities of the country entering a recession, but at Arizona Computer Outlets things were very different. New customers were coming in based on referrals alone, profits were up, and expenses were down. February 2008 was our best month ever, even beating the month we bought the store!

The store's net revenue had increased almost 90 percent from the July 2007 lows and the store turned a profit of almost $7,000 in February 2008. Sales were now in the pipeline and on the last day of February, we had $25,000 in sales ready to be closed in March. We had turned our business around and two years later, in July of 2009, we expanded to a second location.

This book documents the lessons learned from hundreds of hours of research and experimentation. It summarizes the advice and examples of other successful small-business owners as well as our own experiences. This book outlines exactly what you need to do to stay afloat in a difficult market. With tried and true methodologies to increase sales and improve customer service, you can grow your business even in tough times.

Many small businesses are still facing economic challenges, but you can turn your business around and successfully navigate through these troubled waters. Once you do, you will be well positioned to take advantage of the next economic boom. Remember, no storm can last forever. In the past, companies that have made it through difficult economic times have often gone on to become significant players when the market improved.

When your business is struggling, work on building, changing, and growing your business. Remember your goal: You wanted more or you wouldn't have bothered starting your business in the first place. Your small business can become the stable, profitable company that you want it to be.

Take a moment to relax and think about how things started. Remember back to the day you first dreamed of having your own business. Think about the anticipation you felt when you decided that you were going to do it. At that time, you probably knew a few people who owned a store or company and they were very successful. But they didn't start out that way: they were all just average people who wanted something better and worked hard to get it.

When you remember back, you probably think about the success you anticipated, the loyal customers, the brand you would create, your picture on the cover of *Entrepreneur* magazine, and most of all, the financial freedom! More than anything else, those goals were what you were trying to achieve and that lifestyle is what you wanted as your reward.

Your goals for your business are what drive you every day. This is why you go to work each morning and why you keep your business open during the tough times. This is the dream that you wish to achieve, the security you will provide for your family, and the freedom you will enjoy.

One of the biggest challenges you will face is figuring out what the best route is to achieve your goals. When you first started, you may have created plans, products, and processes that were designed to grow your business. However, as your business grew, you may have discovered that you had to dramatically change things in order to keep your business running.

As you read this book, you may find it challenging to replace your existing ideas with new ones. In our business, change was one of our challenges. It wasn't until we were faced with almost losing our business that we realized we had to change to survive.

In order to make the changes your business needs, you have to be brutally honest with yourself. As a small-business owner, you have made hundreds of decisions to get your business up and running smoothly. Now, it is time to review each of those decisions. It's hard, but you need to choose which ideas are working and which aren't. For some people, this may be the most difficult part, but if you can commit to redesigning your business, changing what doesn't work, and committing to what you have done well, you will be on your way to turning your business around.

With advice from many small-business owners who have survived difficult times and are still successful, you will have the knowledge and power to change your course, succeed, and reach your goals. Before you begin, take a moment, close your eyes, and imagine what your life will become when the business is growing and successful and you reach your goals.

In the following chapters, we will present 19 ways to help ensure you're successful in this tough economy. We wrote down a list of things that helped us and other small-business owners remain successful and narrowed it down to the ones we felt were absolutely critical for success. Most of these, if ignored, could lead to the loss of your business. When the economy is booming, it's easy to slack off, but that time has passed. The time to act is now, not when you're facing financial ruin. It's time to make a choice. You can turn back and give up your dream or buckle down, press on, and succeed. An unknown, wise person once said, "A bend in the road is not the end of the road ... unless you fail to make the turn."

1
COMMIT TO MAKING YOUR BUSINESS A SUCCESS

As the owner of a business, you are in a unique position. You have already devoted your time, resources, and energy to creating and growing your company. When the challenges of a tough economy occur, it can seem frustrating, as conditions beyond your control start to erode the strong foundation you have built. For example, customers may order less because the overflowing budgets they used to have no longer exist.

To make matters worse, even if you want to leave your business, that doesn't mean the stress will go away. Folding a company is sometimes as difficult as starting. You have to decide how to leave, what to sell, what to negotiate and in the end, you may still be left with a lot of debt and possibly even continuing expenses.

Many small-business owners waste time when their business starts to wane trying to decide what to do next. Instead of solving the problems and facing the new challenges, they waste their time thinking about whether or not they should get out. They sometimes second-guess whether they should own the business at all.

Some owners go as far as to research how to sell the business (which can be difficult and require a great deal of financial preparation), or even worse, they immediately look for a job outside the business to make ends meet. In the end, these tactics stretch already strained resources. There are plenty of examples of successful businesspeople who only achieved success following many failures; for instance, Walt Disney went bankrupt before the Disney we know today succeeded.

However, it is not possible to execute two opposite plans effectively — the company must have only one direction and it is necessary for you, the owner, to decide which direction to choose. Commit, succeed, and grow; or quit, fail, and close. You can't do both.

1. You Can't Learn to Swim in a Classroom

Think back to how you learned to swim, ride a bike, or catch a ball. These activities require active participation and can't be learned in a classroom. While it is possible to memorize the state capitals without visiting each one, no one would every claim to be able to swim without having been in the water. To learn any activity you have to start somewhere — usually by just trying it. You may have had someone helping you who was able to give you advice, show you what you were doing wrong, and prevent you from getting hurt, but for the most part, it was up to you to learn from your experience.

Let's be fair — you don't learn new skills immediately. For most of us, we didn't get the hang of swimming on our first try in the water, or our second try, or even our third try. Instead, it probably took quite a while to learn to swim and even longer to master the various strokes. However, this is expected, and understood. For most of us, learning any new skill requires patience and practice. Very few people become experts at anything without a few failures under their belt. Failure, however, is part of the path to success and very little is learned without it.

2. It's Okay to Fail Sometimes

For some reason, we are repeatedly taught not to fail. In our schools and in our jobs, risks are generally discouraged. If a risk doesn't result in an immediate success, we are condemned as having failed. When you were in school, the questions were generally straightforward and someone (usually the teacher) always had a simple, correct answer. Later, as you left school and went into the business world, you may have found that large companies have a very similar philosophy. The jobs are very well defined, the processes are usually documented, and your boss usually has rigid ideas about how everything should be done.

As if that weren't enough, since many large companies are on the stock exchange, stringent government regulations usually mean the company has massive policy and process documents that each employee is expected to follow. Just as schoolchildren are expected to get the "right" answer, if an employee fails to get the right answer or follow a detailed rule, he or she is immediately condemned for not completing the task correctly.

The world of schoolchildren and employees is not the same as that of business owners. After you become a business owner, these archaic rules are turned on their head. Very often, what makes a business successful is an owner who is willing to fail; what makes a business a failure is an owner who won't take any chances.

3. Risks Lead to Rewards

Business owners that profit the most are usually those who take the largest risks and are willing to accept failure. Most small businesses that grow to become large companies started with an idea or product that was unusual and had owners that took a risk.

In 1978, two small-business owners started a homemade ice cream shop after taking a $5 ice cream making correspondence course from Penn State University. They were able to start their business with $12,000 and somehow were even able to borrow $4,000 of that money. Many people would not have invested in such an unorthodox business, especially with two owners that were obviously building it in an unusual way. However, the company turned into one of the most well known names in ice cream: Ben & Jerry's.[1]

---

[1] Ben & Jerry's, "Press Release — Ben & Jerry's Chunk Fest," http://www.benjerry.com.sg/moopress/081119_chunkfest.pdf (November 9, 2008).

There are many success stories like this throughout large companies and they all trace their roots back to entrepreneurs that were willing to take a chance, make mistakes, and learn from their experiences. It is impossible for any owner to grow his or her business, try new things, and never fail.

4. Mistakes Mean You Are Learning

In order to be successful it will be necessary for you to be willing to adapt and learn. Unfortunately, the only way to learn is to find a problem and try to solve it. When you fail, you have the opportunity to learn. Every mistake you make shows that you stepped up to a problem and ran into a situation you weren't expecting. It is only then that you have the opportunity to learn from that experience.

If you're going to grow, you must expect to recreate and redesign your business over and over to adapt to various market conditions. Today's problems may be different than yesterday's, and nothing like tomorrow's. Throughout the journey of owning a business you will find that some decisions you make yield poor results while others are more profitable than you ever expected. Just be prepared to make mistakes, learn from those mistakes, and use those experiences to become even more successful.

Lifesaver: If you don't already have one, purchase a day planner. Day planners allow you to organize your ideas and track your progress. There are planners that fit almost any style or need. Make sure to choose one that fits your lifestyle to ensure that you will use it daily.

5. Commit to Success

Although it may be difficult during a business downturn, commitment to your goals is more critical than ever. Customers and clients like to work with companies that are successful. Employees like to work for companies that are successful. If your business is in trouble, and if you want it to survive, you need to commit to making the business succeed. It is when a business begins to struggle that focus, dedication, and hard work are needed the most. Spreading yourself among many different solutions will ensure that, at best, you accomplish some of them poorly.

When we were facing issues with our own business, we often discussed "outside" solutions. Should we sell the business? Should we close the doors and walk away? Would we be better off hiring a manager to run it and just go back to a "real job"? At one point, we realized that as long as we considered outside solutions like these, we weren't committing fully to our business. One day, we decided that we were not going to entertain the option of failing any longer. All conversations we were going to have about the business would be about how to improve and grow the business. To be fair, we also gave it a time limit. If our efforts did not show positive improvement in three months, we would then consider other options, but only then and only after we had fully dedicated ourselves to improving our store. The results were amazing. By committing time and resources to the store, we found that we were able to accomplish a great deal more.

If you hesitate, your lack of dedication will begin to permeate your organization. Employees may feel that if you aren't committed they should not be committed. Oftentimes, if employees hear than an owner is considering leaving the business or closing, they begin to look for other employment in an attempt to obtain job security. One salon owner we know ran into this very situation. When her business started to fail she confided in her manager that she was considering selling the business. Within a few short months her manager found another full-time position. Although the salon owner hadn't finalized a sale, she lost her best employee and was still going under. Similarly, customers who question how long a business will remain open may be more likely to go to a competitor. When the owner is uncommitted, it is noticed by those around him or her and this domino effect can have a profoundly negative impact on the entire organization.

However, if you show that you are committed to your business, services, customers, and employees, it will be felt throughout your organization. When employees know you are dedicated to working through tough times they will be willing to stay onboard, and may accept the challenges of working through the tough times more willingly than you may imagine.

The excitement of taking on a new challenge, overcoming obstacles, and succeeding in the face of failure is enticing. Many employees are most excited when their company is taking on challenges and winning. The idea of succeeding, even when a new megastore moves in next door, or of watching your competitors fold as times get leaner is appealing. Even though your employees do not own the company or necessarily profit by its success, everyone enjoys being part of a winning team. By committing to your own success, you can bring that excitement to your company and your employees.

Lifesaver: Being a business owner is a round the clock job. Unfortunately, the time you put in working at home and running errands is time that your employees can't see. Let your employees know how much time you spend both at the job and at home working for the business. Letting them know how many hours you put in each week is a tangible way to show them your commitment to the business.

6. Control Your Business

A small company needs to be controlled by its owners. Opinions will abound; however, the company vision and direction need to be set by the owners who are responsible for it. If this is left to employees in the organization, the result can often be a mishmash of conflicting directions and objectives.

This does not mean that every task must be completed by you and it doesn't mean that you have to be the best at every task. Taking control is not about doing all the work, but about realizing that if the work isn't done right, in the end, the responsibility falls on your shoulders. As the business owner, you must determine what tasks are most important and make sure they are done correctly and completely. If things aren't done right, you are the only one to blame.

7. Communicate Your Goals Clearly

What is your vision of your company? What does success look like? What are you doing well? What are you not doing well? Before you can expect your team to help you meet your goals, you need to know what you want and be prepared to describe how to get there. This book is filled with ideas and solutions that business owners have used to grow their businesses, increase their revenue, and build their customer base. You will have to choose which ideas you want to implement, and when. Then, you will have to communicate these goals to your employees and make sure they are executed effectively.

It is not enough to tell employees, "This store is always messy." You must be a proactive communicator who can provide instructions as well as constructive criticism. Providing detailed goals and objectives even in small tasks will help your employees know what you want and understand how to get there. Your team needs to understand what your goals are, how to achieve them, and why they are important.

To do this, first explain your goal, and be positive. It has been found that using negatives to instruct individuals causes people to miss the message. For instance, if you say, "This place is trashed — what a disaster!," people tend to fixate on the fact that the store is messy, which is a negative concept. Wording the phrase in a positive way tends to have more impact, for instance, "This store needs to be clean and well ordered. Customers will enjoy it more." In this case, you are focusing yourself and your team on the results you want to achieve and direction you want to go. Affirming positive goals and ideals is more effective then dwelling on problems and shortcomings.

Next, provide clear examples of how you expect the goal to be achieved. For instance you can say, "Please make sure the floor is vacuumed every night before closing." This very specific instruction lets your team know exactly what you expect from them, and when

you expect it to be completed. Although this sounds simplistic it ensures that you are clearly stating how you expect the team to achieve these goals. You cannot assume that everyone has a vision of how to achieve the goals just because it is obvious to you. The more up-front you are the less likely there is to be confusion.

Lastly, explain why you want these tasks completed and why it is important; for example, "Having a clean store is more comfortable for the customers and will lead to more sales." Adding why you want something accomplished lets your team know that you have a goal in mind that will benefit the business. No one likes busywork. If possible, always try to include how the business revenue will increase with this change. By making your changes about increasing sales revenue, the team will start to realize that a business is about servicing customers and everything a business does should encourage revenue.

Lifesaver: As you are redesigning your organization, you will find many opportunities for improvement. Unfortunately, you will be unable to execute all the ideas at the same time. Some tasks cannot or should not be completed immediately. Add these items to your planner in future months, or just a few weeks ahead. This will give you the ability to remember the great ideas, without letting them get in the way of your current tasks.

8. Lead by Example

As the business owner, you are in a unique position. You are the highest authority in the company and have the final say on any decision that occurs. Therefore, your values and your beliefs will permeate the organization. Each decision you make influences your employees' decision making. If they know you support a particular way of doing something, they will be more comfortable making similar decisions. Contrarily, if they know you oppose something, your employees will be unlikely to want to risk their job by opposing your rules or values.

Therefore, the fastest and most efficient way to change any organization is to exemplify the values and ideals you want your employees to follow. If you want employees to put extra hours in when a customer needs help, you must be the first person to volunteer to stay and complete the task. If you want your customers to receive great service, you must go out of your way for each patron you deal with. If you want your business expenses to go down, you must cut your own costs, reduce spending, and let your team know that frugal decisions are valued. The more your team has the ability to observe your values and the way your decisions are made, the faster they will learn what needs to be done and how to do it.

Of course, leading your business shouldn't be limited to leading your employees. As a business owner, you need to make yourself visible and available to your customers and clients. It is equally important for them to see your company's values. When you back up your company's warranties and guarantee the workmanship, from whom are the customers really buying? From you! After all, if the owner stands behind his or her company, the customer will feel that any problem can be resolved and any wrong will be made right.

Most businesses aren't likely to grow to stardom when the owner is uninvolved and uncommitted. If you think of any successful business — Microsoft, Berkshire Hathaway, Disney — you can usually name the committed business owner behind its rise to stardom: Bill Gates, Warren Buffett, and Walt Disney. Similarly, your commitment and dedication can drive your business to grow and be profitable.

2

COMPLY WITH ALL GOVERNMENT RULES AND REGULATIONS

In business, government rules can be complicated and unclear, but they exist —and if you want your company to be successful, you better follow them. If you ignore government rules and regulations, you could jeopardize your business. With this in mind, before your company can begin to grow, you must first ensure that you don't have any restrictions holding you back. For a company, these restrictions can take many forms. There could be government licenses that are not properly in place, fees and interest charges that are increasing, or regulations that are not being obeyed. Each of these areas need to be reviewed and resolved to ensure that the work you put into growing your business will not be in vain. There is no point in building a business only to have the tax people come in and seize all your assets. With a little preventative maintenance you can ensure that your business can grow and flourish.

1. Protecting Your Personal Assets

Years ago, when exploration was young and trade was booming, Europeans would send out ships to distant lands to open new routes and develop new business opportunities. However, when something went wrong, such as losing a ship and with it the cargo and lives of the sailors, the individuals that set up the voyage could become liable. This meant that their personal interests would be used to pay for the losses that were incurred. Unfortunately, this type of risk is too significant for anyone with any accumulated assets to take. If a ship was lost at sea, the individual's home, business, and livelihood would all be risked. Therefore, to reduce this risk and encourage exploration, corporations were developed.

Corporations function the same way today as they did back when they were first created.

Incorporating allows the business to become its own legal entity, which means individuals can invest in a new venture, but limit their risk to the money they have invested in that business.

If you are running your business as a sole proprietorship, even if you are the only employee, you are risking all of your personal assets if the business is held liable. To protect yourself, make sure that you are properly incorporated. Check with your accountant or lawyer to help determine the best business structure for your situation.

 **Lifesaver:** There are a few different types of entities you can choose from when you incorporate. The type of entity you choose can impact your tax obligations. Make sure to talk with a qualified tax professional about the tax advantages of each type of incorporation before you choose one. The decision you make could save you a significant amount of money on your taxes.

After you have a properly incorporated business, make sure you run it as a business. This means that you must follow your state or province's requirements regarding the organization and operation of a corporation. Although it may seem unnecessary, it is important that you hold the appropriate meetings and file the annual paperwork if required. Depending where your business is located and the type of incorporation you choose, these obligations can vary so make sure to work with an experienced professional to set up and manage your company.

Sometimes business owners are tempted to let their personal finances mix with their business finances. Once this happens, it can create all sorts of risks for the owners. The least of which is the tax risk associated with misallocated resources. If you are audited, your deductions can be rejected if they were not legitimately associated with your business. However, the bigger risk comes if your company is ever sued and found liable. If you do not keep your business and personal finances separate, it could be sufficient proof that you have not formally provided enough separation between yourself and the business. Once this is established, you can be held personally accountable for the liabilities of the business. Your personal assets, home, car, and investments will now be available to provide restitution for whatever financial award is decided.

To ensure you have properly separated your personal and business assets, there are a few simple things that you should do:

- Ensure your business is properly incorporated and maintains its incorporation status. Depending on the state or province in which you file, there are various rules that must be adhered to in order for a business to maintain its incorporation. If you aren't sure how to do this, make sure you engage the services of a professional.

- Obtain and use a business Employee Identification Number (EIN) in the United States or a Business Number (BN) in Canada. These business numbers function similar to a social security number or social insurance number and are used for business bank accounts, tax identification, and lines of credit.

- Maintain separate finances. Each corporation that you own should have its own bank account. Further, financial transactions that occur in that account should be limited to those activities and purchases that are related to the business only.

- File business taxes. Your business should always file its own taxes using its own EIN or BN. Talk to a tax professional to make sure that this is done properly.

Of course, these guidelines are just recommendations. To ensure that you are in compliance with Federal, state, or provincial guidelines, regularly check with your lawyer or accountant. It will always be less expensive and easier to pay for advice up front rather than deal with the penalties later.

2. Set up Your Business Credit

Even if you have a business properly set up, you may find that you have to personally sign for credit for your business. If you have co-signed with your business, you are personally responsible for that line of credit. Eventually, if your business grows enough, there is an alternative to personally signing for credit. It is possible for a business to build its own credit rating and get its own line of credit. This type of credit can also be used to expand credit to vendors and to purchase goods and services from suppliers.

In the same way that individuals can monitor their personal credit, business credit can also be monitored. The leading agency for business credit monitoring is Dun & Bradstreet (D&B). Once you sign up with D&B you will receive a unique nine-digit sequence (D-U-N-S Number), which will begin establishing your credit history. Like your personal credit rating, this business credit rating can be used by other businesses to check how creditworthy your company really is. Therefore, keep an eye on this rating. If there are any erroneous items, make sure you dispute them as quickly as possible. Keeping this record accurate is an important part of ensuring your business's creditworthiness.

3. Taxes

In order to keep your business going in a tough economy, you have to keep up with your taxes. You also would be wise to take advantage of tax deductions and to protect yourself from future tax problems.

3.1 Get every tax deduction possible

Once you have properly incorporated your business, work with your accountant to make sure you are aware of what legitimate business expenses you should be deducting from your business income. As a business owner, you will find that many common expenses are now recognized as legitimate business expenses. Basically, if the expense incurred is part of doing business, it can be deducted. Although this sounds like a very simple rule, there are amazingly detailed and complex applications.

The Internal Revenue Service (IRS) and Canada Revenue Agency (CRA) have numerous publications on the topic of tax deductions and there are many books, websites, and articles dedicated to ensuring that you know how to take as many tax deductions as you are allowed. Take some time and become familiar with what you can and cannot deduct in your particular line of business. You may be surprised how many deduction opportunities are available.

One good book to read on US taxes is *Tax This! An Insider's Guide to Standing up to the IRS*, written by the former tax attorney Scott M. Estill, and published by Self-Counsel Press.

3.2 The high cost of not paying your taxes

When businesses are stretched thin, one of the more common bills to fall behind on is the tax bill. As a small-business owner, you probably have found that there are many different types of taxes that you are now obligated to collect and pay. However, unlike your electric bill, when you get behind on your tax bills, there is no immediate consequence. The first month you don't pay your electric bill you may get a late notice. A month or so later the electric company may threaten to turn off your electric service and just a short time after that, you will lose your electricity. For business owners, this immediate impact is very concrete. Since almost all companies need electricity to stay open, the electric bill is usually paid. Most other bills, such as rent, cable, telephone, and employee salaries are very similar. After all, how long would your employees remain with your company if they were no longer getting paid? The tax bill, however, is quite different. When taxes are unpaid the consequences are much less noticeable at first.

3.2a US tax consequences

In the US, if you are behind on your employees' payroll taxes (i.e., money that comes out of the employees' paychecks to pay income tax, social security, and Medicare), and have only been paying the employees their after-tax salaries, you may end up paying a penalty. This means that you never filed or paid the employees' payroll taxes. At first, there won't appear to be any problem. In the beginning all the Internal Revenue Service (IRS) will do is send out letters indicating that the taxes have not been filed. Unlike the electric bill, there is nothing to threaten to shut off. If you are a business owner short on cash, this may seem like an easy letter to ignore. However, if you have chosen to ignore your taxes and not file, you are creating a significant issue.

In the US, when taxes aren't filed, the government can add a penalty to your tax bill of 5 percent every month, up to 25 percent of your bill. For example, you owe $5,000, and don't have the money to pay. If you choose to file when you have the money six months later, you will now owe the original $5,000 plus an additional $1,250 penalty, which is 25 percent of the original bill. In addition, every month this bill accumulates interest. If the taxes have been filed, and even a small amount had been paid (e.g., only $1,000), the only penalty the business would have to pay would be a reasonable interest fee on the amount still owed.

Now let's say that the business fails to file taxes for an extended period and ignores all the notifications received. Eventually the IRS will take notice and act aggressively. The IRS has a great deal of liberty with what it can actually do to get the money it is owed. If taxes are not paid, and if your business is not making any effort to pay, the IRS can take drastic action. The IRS can ask the taxpayer to sell or mortgage assets, take out a loan, or even take more aggressive steps. The IRS can take "enforced collection actions" such as levying bank accounts, garnishing wages, or simply seizing assets such as the money in your bank account. Further, the IRS can also file a "Notice of Federal Tax Lien" that could have a negative impact on your credit standing.[1] By now, the business will not only owe all of the taxes and penalties, but the costs for accountants and lawyers to respond to the charges can begin to pile up. Even filing bankruptcy is not protection from the IRS. In some cases, such as the payroll tax example used here, this debt would not be eliminated by bankruptcy. The government considers this money "employee" money, so your failure to file and pay is considered theft!

---

[1] Internal Revenue Service, "Filing Late and/or Paying Late," http://www.irs.gov/businesses/small/article/0,,id=108326,00.html (May 2009).

3.2b Resolving tax issues in the USA

If you realize that your business is already behind on taxes, there are ways to resolve a back tax issue without losing control of the situation in the US. The best way to start is to work with a reputable accountant immediately to determine your business's debt and options. Allowing a professional accountant to examine the situation may result in better options than if you try to resolve the situation alone. Although you will have to pay for your accountant's time, the recommendations he or she provides may save you more money than what you spent.

If you know what your business owes, and you believe that your company may be able to pay the majority of the bill, you may just want to call the Internal Revenue Service (IRS). The IRS offers ways to pay off your debt without risking your business. Some options include setting up monthly payments, or negotiating to reduce the amount of debt, also known as an Offer In Compromise (OIC) settlement. The IRS also accepts credit card payments, so it is possible to pay off your tax bill on a credit card and then pay down the credit card over a longer period of time than the IRS would typically allow.

In some cases, accountants may be able to petition on your behalf to reduce the penalties and interest due to extenuating circumstances. If you think that your business may qualify for this assistance, you may want to contact a Local Taxpayer Advocate. This is an independent organization within the IRS that reports to the National Taxpayer Advocate. Each state has at least one Local Taxpayer Advocate. These advocates are free, independent, and confidential. They typically work to assist taxpayers — both individuals and businesses —who are unable to resolve their tax issues through normal channels or who are experiencing a hardship.[2]

> # WARNING:
> Be careful of businesses that claim they can help negotiate tax bills. While some of these companies are legitimate, others prey on people in trouble. They will ask for thousands of dollars up front and then be unable to reduce the debt. In general, contact your own accountant or lawyer for assistance or for a reputable referral.

Occasionally, you may be lucky enough to take advantage of amnesty programs. These programs can be either at the Federal, state, or local level. The programs usually require you to pay all of the outstanding debt that you owe, but they will waive the penalties and interest charges that you incurred by not paying on time. For some taxpayers the extra charges can amount to thousands of dollars. For instance, in February 2009, the Massachusetts Department of Revenue offered 159,000 tax delinquents amnesty if they paid their debts by April, 2009. Later that same year, Arizona passed two amnesty programs for their State and City Transaction Privilege Taxes (i.e., Sales Tax). Each of these programs varied in its implementation, duration, and applicability but it encouraged business owners to file and pay the tax they owed with either reduced or eliminated penalties and interest.

Beware, some amnesty programs don't just offer a benefit, they also punish those

---

[2] Internal Revenue Service, "Contact a Local Taxpayer Advocate," http://www.irs.gov/advocate/content/0,,id=150972,00.html (May 2009).

that don't take advantage of the opportunity to resolve their tax bill. In 2005, the state of California offered an amnesty program that ran from February to March of 2005. The program covered California corporate franchise tax, personal income tax, sales tax, and use taxes for pre-2003 periods. If a taxpayer participated in the program, the individual or business would have amnesty — no criminal or financial penalties would be incurred. The company could simply pay the tax owed and nothing more. However, taxpayers who did not participate in the program and who owed tax would be penalized. If they did not take advantage of the program, file their missing taxes, and pay off their debt, they could now be fined even more heavily than they were before. Missing the amnesty program could now result in a 40 percent accuracy-related penalty, doubling the sales tax penalties plus an automatic 50 percent penalty surcharge on interest![3]

Whichever course you choose, be sure to handle unresolved tax issues as quickly as possible. Since the government is entitled to this money, it can take extreme measures to get its funds. As a business owner, you don't want to check your accounts one day to find that your assets have been seized and all the cash has been suddenly removed from your bank account. The impact this could have on a business would be devastating. Without money in the bank, chances are your business would be unable to purchase more products, pay your bills, or even pay your employees. Most businesses can resolve their back tax issues. Taking control and resolving it with the IRS is a much better, safer option than ignoring it and allowing the government to simply choose when and how to handle the problem. The sooner these problems are solved the better.

Lifesaver: While resolving back tax issues, make sure to keep filing and paying your current taxes on time. This will both ensure that you don't incur additional fines and will give you more credibility when you start paying down your older bills. In some cases, the tax agency may even be willing to remove your most recent fines since you have been staying current with your tax debts.

3.2c Canadian tax consequences

In Canada, if you haven't filed or paid your employees' payroll taxes — that is, money that comes out of the employees' paychecks to pay income tax, Canadian Pension Plan (CPP), and Employment Insurance (EI) — and have only been paying the employees their after-tax salaries, you may end up paying a penalty.

It won't take long before Canada Revenue Agency (CRA) sends you a letter indicating that the payroll taxes have not been filed. This may seem like an easy letter to ignore; however, if you choose to ignore your taxes and not file, you will have a big problem.

CRA may assess a penalty of 10 percent of the required amount you failed to deduct for income tax, CPP, and EI. If you fail to file again in a calendar year, CRA may apply a 20 percent penalty, especially if you knowingly made the decision to not deduct the payroll taxes. You could also be fined $1,000 to $25,000 or be imprisoned for up to a year.

3.2d Relief for penalties and interest on taxes in Canada

If you realize that your business is already behind on taxes, there are ways to resolve a back

---

[3] California State Board of Equalization, "Special Notice: Tax Amnesty — Related Penalties and Billing Time Limits," http://www.boe.ca.gov/news/pdf/sntaxamnesty.pdf (November 2005).

tax issue without losing control of the situation. The best way to start is to work with a reputable accountant immediately to determine your business's debt and options. Allowing a professional accountant to examine the situation may result in better options than if you try to resolve the situation alone. Although you will have to pay for your accountant's time, the recommendations he or she provides may save you more money than what you spent.

You may be able to have your penalties and interest waived or cancelled in the following situations:[4]

- Extraordinary circumstance, which means something out of your control prevented you from paying your taxes on time (e.g., flood, fire, postal strike, serious accident or illness, or death in the immediate family).

- Inability to pay or a financial hardship. In this case, if accumulated interest causes prolonged financial hardship to the point that basic necessities cannot be provided such as medical help, food, transportation, or shelter.

- Actions by the Canadian Revenue Agency (CRA), such as processing delays that prevent a taxpayer being informed in a timely manner about an amount owing, errors in information given to the public that caused errors in the taxes filed, incorrect information provided to tax payers, errors in processing, delays in providing information, or delays in completing an audit.

If you fall into any of these categories, you may be able to get relief. You or your accountant can write to the CRA and ask that your penalties and interest be waived or cancelled.

In some circumstances you may still have to pay the interest, but the CRA will reduce the amount.

3.3 Prevent tax problems in the future

The easiest way to prevent tax problems in the future is to always file and pay your taxes on time. If you are like many small-business owners, the management overhead of a business is often very time-consuming. Mundane tasks, such as paying taxes, can easily be forgotten when the business is busy. To ensure that you are staying on top of your taxes, set up a regular schedule for payments. If possible, outsource the work to a bookkeeper or an accounting service. Although the cost of these services may seem expensive, these vendors typically guarantee on-time, accurate filings. Since the cost of late payments is so significant, if you think you could be late even once throughout the year, you may save more money by hiring an outside vendor than you would by trying to file all of your taxes yourself.

 **Lifesaver:** Although tax agencies still accept paper forms, many tax offices now allow businesses to pay taxes online. Some agencies even have automated forms that calculate the tax due. Filing online also ensures that you will never have to worry about the mail being lost or experiencing a delay due to office processing. The day you submit is the day your taxes are filed.

4. Follow Regulations and Rules

In almost every business, there are government, state or provincial, and local regulations that you must adhere to. Failure to follow these

---

[4] CRA, "Taypayer Relief Provisions," http://www.cra-arc.gc.ca/gncy/frnss/prv_2-eng.html (May 31, 2007).

rules can result in anything from small, manageable fines, to suddenly having your business closed down. Unfortunately, as each area has different rules, it is often difficult to determine just what obligations your business has. Further, if your business completes sales in more than one state or province, you will need to be familiar with the laws of all the states or provinces where you do business.

Of course, the laws are not simple. The details surrounding legal decisions can seem unreasonably specific in many cases. Let's say for example that you are the owner of a mobile vending business doing business in Arizona and you want to determine if soda is taxable. The state of Arizona actually has a specific guideline about what types of foods are taxable by mobile vendors. Further, when you look into this guideline you would find that soda can be either taxable or nontaxable depending on how it is sold. If it is being sold by a mobile vendor in a cup or open container (e.g., a fountain soda), the drink is fully taxable as the soda is considered food for consumption on the premises. If the soda is prepackaged (e.g., in a can or bottle), then it is considered a nontaxable product, which means it is not considered food for consumption on the premises. As if that weren't specific enough, there is an additional ruling added to this guideline that food items sold in any venue that charges admission (e.g., bowling alleys, sports venues) are taxable.[5] Subtle distinctions like these, if applicable, can be important to your business. Therefore, each rule needs to be understood thoroughly.

There are a few simple ways to get this information. The most direct is to approach your state or provincial and local government and simply ask what obligations your business has.

Unfortunately since these government officials will not be familiar with all the specifics of your business, there are times when the advice you receive from these officials may not be accurate or may be out of date. As a result, you should always follow up with other business owners or the Small Business Association (SBA) to find out how these rules really apply.

5. Post All Required Notices

Make sure to check your state or provincial and local business regulations for any notice you are required to post or display. According to US Federal law there are a handful of Federal notices that you are required to display. For instance, if you have employees, there are federal forms that must be posted such as the "Federal Minimum Wage Notice." Failure to post the required messages could result in financial penalties and other legal consequences. Similarly, states and provinces often obligate businesses to post certain notices, and the required documentation depends where your business is located. Take some time to research what notifications are required in your area.

Aside from these notices, you may find that there are licenses that you have to obtain. In some cases, these licenses are also supposed to be posted prominently. Since these may vary based on your type of business, you should check the federal, state or provincial, and local offices that regulate your business. Also, make sure to include any notices that may be valuable disclaimers. For instance, if you run a food-service establishment that offers raw (e.g., sushi) or undercooked food on the menu (e.g., medium-rare steaks), you may need to include a menu disclaimer that describes the risks of eating undercooked food.

---

[5] Arizona Department of Revenue, "Arizona Transaction Privilege Tax Ruling," http://www.azdor.gov (July 2002).

6. Forms, Documentation, and Disclaimers

Another way to protect your business interests is to ensure that you document what your business does. Instead of trying to create new forms for your business, it is faster and more efficient to get premade forms that can be used by your business. Having some of your day-to-day activities formally documented is helpful as it allows you to have a written history of what your business did and when it was done.

Documentation may be helpful if you ever need to check the history of a customer order, track a purchase, or document an employee termination. This backup documentation is very useful if you ever have a customer issue that has escalated. For instance, once, we had a customer who was dissatisfied with her service. She claimed that she was unaware of the risks associated with fixing an old, failing computer. Instead of telling someone at the store so that it could be resolved, she paid, left quietly, and took the issue directly to the Better Business Bureau (BBB). Having a strong documentation trail allowed us to settle the problem to everyone's satisfaction. We were able to provide the BBB with the documents they needed to see that we had in fact notified her of all her risks and issues. We attached her signed check-in form that clearly showed we had outlined the risks associated with repairing a damaged computer like hers. We then worked with the customer to make her happy and to retain her business.

Disclaimers are a good way to protect your business and they can also provide opportunities for additional sales. For instance, at most car dealerships the salesperson will review the warranty paperwork with the customer. At this point, when the limitations of the warranty are being discussed (e.g., only 3 years), the salesperson has a perfect opportunity to offer the customer an extended warranty.

If you don't already have documents in place, they are easy to find or purchase. Self-Counsel Press publishes *Small Business Forms*; a kit that contains a CD with the forms typically used by small businesses to complete their day-to-day operations including personnel forms (e.g., employee performance reviews, employment applications), financial forms (e.g., invoices, statements, purchase orders), and even general office forms (e.g., memos, telephone messages). Obtaining a low cost premade package like this saves time that you can better use to grow your business.

Another type of document you will need if you are providing a customer service such as repair work or consulting advice is a standard service contract that can be used with your customers. This contract should include the possible negative outcomes (e.g., damage) that could occur and the limits around your company's liability. Legal forms can be purchased at your local software vendor or on the Internet. For extra safety have your company's lawyer review the document before you use it. It may be necessary to draft a customer form for your specific business needs.

7. Finding Reliable Information

By now, you may be starting to be concerned that it will be difficult, if not impossible to keep up with the many government, state or provincial, local, municipal, and city rules. Fortunately, there is a way to stay compliant with all the various rules, regulations, notices, obligations, and laws that are out there.

The US government has a site called Business.Gov that helps your business navigate its way through the maze of state, federal, and local laws. This site is designed to help small business understand their legal requirements and to find the appropriate services. This is an official site of the US government that provides links to other resources throughout the federal, state, and local government. It effectively helps organize the resources that are available to make it easier on business owners. If you aren't sure where to start looking for information on your issue, this is a great place to begin. Some of the items available at this site include easy-to-find links to information businesses need on topics such as taxes, financing, grants, state compliance, industry compliance, local laws, specific industry rules, and much more. This site is a fantastic resource for business owners and their employees.

Canada Business (www.canadabusiness.ca) and Industry Canada (www.ic.gc.ca) offer helpful information and links on their websites. On these sites, business owners can find information about taxes, laws, regulations, and permits, among many other helpful topics.

3
ELIMINATE THE FINANCIAL OBSTACLES

When managing a business, in any type of market, it is vital to track expenses. However, in a tough economy, even the smallest financial waste can quickly destroy your profitability. The business owner and the employees have to understand that eliminating unnecessary expenses isn't something they should get to when they have a free minute, after lunch, or when Simmons in accounting gets back from vacation. Any financial leak needs to be plugged as soon as it's found, before it's too late.

Most company owners value and understand the importance of having a complete financial picture of their company. Unfortunately, when the business is struggling, some business owners don't take the time to review their company's entire financial picture. Instead they focus on increasing profitability without cutting expenses. A business needs to be in a strong financial condition to be successful.

What does a successful financial picture look like during turbulent market conditions? From an expense perspective, the company is lean and tight, running on as little money as possible to sustain the success of the business. Ideally, at this point, expenses should be trimmed low enough that income meets or exceeds expenses. If you are trying to turn your business around during an economic downturn, this may appear to be very difficult. Often a struggling company has expenses that significantly exceed their income. By focusing efforts on reducing expenses instead of generating sales, the company will see improvements today, not six months from now. Plus, cutting an expense gives you a recurring advantage. A $500 per month expense you cut is $6,000 per year, whereas a $500 sale is only $500.

The bills must be looked at with a cold and unflinching eye toward reducing expenses and saving you money. Each business expense will need to be reviewed and serious consideration will need to be taken to determine what you can reduce, what you can defer, and what you can eliminate. Of course, all of your expenses cannot simply be eliminated. For each group of expenses, there will be very different methods to reduce the costs. This simple review is the beginning of turning around your business. After all, any money that you are able to shave off of your expenses will bring your business closer to success.

 **Lifesaver:** If you don't already have an accounting program, invest in one. Tracking expenses in a software program will speed monthly sales tax reporting and yearly tax filing. Further, it is easy to create clear reports of the business's financial picture. If you are not comfortable with accounting, hire a bookkeeper or accountant to set up your accounts correctly.

Take special care to review any bills that you don't pay yourself. You may find that even your most trusted managers are not as concerned about your spending as you are. When we reviewed our expenses, we were shocked to discover how high some of our basic bills had escalated. For instance, our store manager was an authorized purchasing agent of the company and he had the authority to order inventory and some other items. He was special-ordering French Vanilla creamers for the staff break room. While this cost was only $40 each month, costs similar to this were adding up and costing our company hundreds of dollars a month. After completing our review, these unnecessary expenses were removed and the company overhead reduced.

The first time you complete your review, you may find that your expenses exceed your income by an unexpected amount. When strong businesses start struggling, it is common for expenses to continue at record highs even when income is declining. Even Fortune 100 companies make this mistake.

If you find that your business is in this situation, the first thing you need to do — before you start expanding your operations, increasing your sales, and saving your business — is to reduce your expenses. Review all the items again and determine what you can reduce or eliminate. Each dollar that is spent without income becomes a debt that your business will have to pay off later. By eliminating as many costs as possible, you reduce the business's operating expenses and when sales start improving, you will become profitable much faster.

1. What Is Your Real Monthly Revenue?

Understanding your net revenue is one of the best ways to begin your financial review. Your net revenue is the gross revenue amount (i.e., the total of all of your sales) minus the cost of goods sold. The cost of your goods can include the cost of the products themselves, the costs of shipping the product, and any other costs for the goods or services you sold. This net revenue allows you to see how much money your business makes *before* the business expenses, such as overhead, salaries, benefits, and other items are paid. In order to understand where you can cut expenses, you must first understand how much money the company actually takes in on a monthly basis.

If you have ever completed a budget for your business or use an accounting program, you will be able to easily find the net revenue for each month. Review these numbers for the last year. What you will probably see is that your monthly net revenue has varied significantly over the last 12 months. Business cycles, vacation periods, and increases in costs all affect the net revenue. In some months your business may have been profitable, in other months, your business may have lost money.

Since you are trying to complete a budget that can work during both difficult and profitable months, use the month with the lowest net revenue in the last 12 months for the budget. This number will be the basis for your budget. Very often owners use averages to run their business expenses. The idea here is that many businesses are cyclical and therefore, one really good month will make up for many bad months. For instance, many retail stores rely on their business making significant sales in December when holiday shoppers abound. However, depending on unusually high months to make a store profitable means that the rest of the year, the store is allowed to either break even or lose money, which is an unsettling way to run a business. If the "big month"doesn't materialize, the company can be in a difficult if not impossible financial position. During December of 2007, many retailers were hit with an unusually slow holiday season. Small businesses were even more affected, as consumers headed to discount stores over "mom and pop" locations. This surprise hit many businesses unexpectedly, greatly reducing their 2007 earnings.

Instead of counting on the best or even an average month, begin to look at your worst month for an indication of how much money your business can make. Using lower than usual net revenue will make your budget estimates much more predictable during difficult financial situations. Even during slow seasons, difficult economic conditions, and unusual market turns, this net revenue amount will represent the approximate amount of income your business can generate. Ideally, all of your expenses should then be reduced to less than this figure. This will create a predictable budget that will allow your business to become profitable as quickly as possible. Instead of losing money during difficult times, your business will be able to sustain itself and focus on growth, not on fighting a losing battle against the mounting debts.

2. Required Expenses versus Desired Expenses

In order to make the best reduction choices for your company you must commit to clearly identifying costs that are *required* versus the costs that are *desired*.

Required business expenses are those expenses that your business cannot survive without. This will be a very short, specific list that includes only those bills that must be paid for your company to remain open. For instance, every business must have the appropriate licenses, and the cost to get licensed can range from the trivial to the exorbitant. The licenses are a good example of critical bills. If you failed to pay them, you would be out of business. This list should not include luxuries that you would like to have to stay in business (e.g., break room coffee service would not be included in this list). Your company can still do business even if it doesn't serve employees free coffee. Therefore, this list should represent only those items that you *must* have to survive.

There are also items that may be required for one business and only desired for another. Items such as rent, utilities, and licensing fees are required for any small store in a strip mall. Without these items, the store couldn't exist. However, if you are working in a consulting business and rarely use an office or you work at home, "rent" may not be on your list, even if you currently have a lease for your business. This list is meant to represent your company's list of only those items that cannot be sacrificed or eliminated.

Now that you understand what to include, go through each bill and determine if each is required or desired. Expenses may include rent; utilities such as water, electricity, and sanitation; insurance; state fees; licenses; phone; Internet; loans; bank fees; and credit card fees. After you total all of these required items, you will have your business's minimum expense list to stay in business. Now compare that number with your lowest net revenue for the last 12 months. If, in your worst month, your revenue isn't higher than the total of your minimum expenses, review your bills again to determine if any expenses can be removed from the required list. Look hard, and remember, nothing is permanent. Anything you drop now can always be added back later. You want to make money *now*, not in two years, so cut deep!

3. Negotiate and Reduce Your Bills

Obviously, since this list represents required business expenses, you cannot reduce your expenses in this area by simply eliminating any of these bills. However, these costs should still be reduced as much as possible so that they represent the minimum spending required on these expenses. Even if you have a contract, signed lease, or recently purchased service, there may still be opportunity to reduce your cost.

First, review each bill on the list and each item on the bill. Just because these bills appear to be required, doesn't mean there aren't any extraneous expenses. For instance, check your local phone bill. Are there any services on the bill that you don't need or use? Are there any items that can be dropped? If you aren't using call-forwarding or three-way calling, why are

you paying for it? Are employees taking advantage of your company and using your phones for personal long distance? Are you paying late fees or penalties? By reducing unnecessary line items on your bills, you can ensure that your overhead contains only necessary costs.

Once you are sure that the bills are correct and the excessive costs are reduced, you may still have the opportunity to reduce your bills further. By researching your options and then negotiating new rates or plans you may be able to lower your costs even more.

 **Lifesaver:** Voice Over IP (VOIP) is one way to get phone service at a much cheaper rate. By running your phone calls over the Internet, providers are able to offer long-distance phone service for much lower rates. In some areas, unlimited long distance can be bundled with your Internet service for as little as $15 per month. This discount can add up to significant savings throughout the year!

Next, for each of the bills on your list, contact any competing vendors. If you do not know any competing vendors, simply go online or check your local phone book. When you call, let the company know you are thinking about switching vendors. Most likely, these competitors will have salespeople available who can help you understand your current bill and your options. In order to ensure that you have the right view of the industry, make sure to get the advice of more than one company. After you have researched competing vendors you will know which provider offers the lowest prices.

If you have found a lower cost provider, make sure to call your original company before you switch. Some companies are competitive and may offer you new enticements to stay. If you haven't found a less expensive option, you may still have some negotiating power with your current vendor. Some business owners find that they have more options after owning a business for a few years than they did when they first started the business. Talk with the sales representatives for each bill and let them know you are shopping around. Sometimes, just bringing this to their attention may make them offer you discounts and services that could be valuable for your company.

Of course, some industries will naturally have more flexibility than others. While your utilities (i.e., water, garbage, and electricity) may not have many competitors, they may have competing packages to review. Other industries, such as insurance, may be very flexible. Insurance, which is often very expensive for a start-up business, may actually decrease as your business continues to have a clean record. Also, the cost of a policy with a higher deductible may be much less expensive than one with a lower deductible.

However, when incidents do occur, you will have to weigh the cost of making a claim and getting some of the money back against not making a claim and paying the costs yourself. Some companies use their insurance regularly to offset the costs of petty theft, vandalism, and damaged goods. While this may resolve the immediate problem, this may not always be financially responsible. Very often, insurance companies will raise your premiums if your company reports too many losses. Unfortunately, one small computer store we know of made four claims in one year. Theft of a laptop, accidental damage to a customer computer, customer file corruption, and a small accident on their property were all settled using their insurance. Although each claim was settled quickly and easily, using insurance that frequently eventually led the insurance company to raise the company's premiums dramatically.

Eventually, the owner closed the business as he claimed the insurance costs alone were making his business unprofitable.

Note that we're not saying that insurance should be eliminated due to the expense. Insurance is an absolute necessity for any small business and cannot be purchased when you need it most (e.g., just after an accident). While you should review your insurance costs your business should not eliminate it.

Lifesaver: Call any company you pay regularly (e.g., insurance carrier, bank, and utility company) and ask about paying with direct debit. Some companies provide discounts to businesses that have automated direct debit set up. Even if they don't offer a discount, you may want to arrange this service. Direct debit can save time on your company's bill payments and save money by eliminating any late fees or penalties.

Approaching your local bank may be another opportunity to reduce your overhead expenses. Banks may be more likely to extend lines of credit to businesses that can show steady sales over the last three to five years. Securing a small business loan may allow you to consolidate debt with higher interest rates in favor of a loan with a lower payment. Another possibility is that some banks may offer better services or reduced charges for companies that do all their business with one bank. Ask a bank manager about small business options and account features.

One of the most difficult costs to change is the cost of your rent. In general, most businesses have a lease that will prevent them from moving without a significant penalty. However, in some cases it may be appropriate to consider moving. For example, an owner of a local store had noticed that improvements were being made to her strip mall location. New trees were planted, a new roof was added, the parking lot was refinished, and many other additions and changes were made. At first she didn't think much about the new modifications; however, the landlord did get her attention when he sent the bill for all the upgrades and new features to each of the tenants. Her company's portion of the renovation came to almost $30,000 in one month. Although she tried to work with the owner and even legally appeal the bill, her lease contract entitled him to recoup the cost of the modifications directly from each tenant. As a result, she moved her business across the street and signed a more reasonable lease with a cap on improvements and repairs.

4. Reduce Unnecessary Employee Expenses

One of the largest expenses for any employer is often the cost of employees. Employees often believe their cost is simply their salaries, but as an owner, it becomes obvious that salary is only one part of the employee expenses. A business owner may find that the costs of his or her employees can greatly exceed the cost of their salary. At some large Fortune 500 companies, the rule of thumb is to take an employee's salary and double it to determine their cost. For small businesses, this multiplier may not be as high, but employee expenses will add up.

To begin determining your employee expenses, include all employees as well as any other individual that works for your company including consultants, interns, temporary help, and bookkeepers. However, do not include yourself in this group even if you work at your business and pay yourself a regular salary. List each of these individuals as well as their salary and any other expense associated with their employment. It may surprise you how many expenses an employee incurs. The following are some employee expenses to include:

- Overtime: Include any money regularly paid for overtime. If this occurs very infrequently, include all estimated overtime costs.

- Bonuses and/or commissions: Include any money provided to an employee as a bonus or commission payment.

- Employment taxes: Include the payroll taxes on each employee's salary and bonuses.

- Benefit premiums: Include any company-sponsored premiums toward insurance, medical, dental, and retirement contributions.

- Benefit management expenses: Include any expenses related to providing the employee benefits. For instance, payroll services, retirement contributions, and management fees.

- Perks: Include the cost of any company perk that is offered. Company perks include any items paid for by the company that are not required by law or as a contracted benefit, including lunches, training, and company phones and cars.

- Meal reimbursement: Include an estimate for reimbursing employees for meals when they are working late.

- Mileage reimbursement: If you regularly reimburse employees for mileage, include an estimate of the monthly amount.

- Management time and expense: If you have any managers responsible for managing your employees, include the estimate of the costs spent on each employee.

- Technology costs: Include the cost of the employee workstations, resources, software licenses, and any other technology-related expenses.

- Workers' Compensation Insurance

Try to make this list as comprehensive as possible so that you can easily see how much each employee actually costs the company.

Although the costs of each person are now in black and white, for many business owners, this is one of the hardest areas in which to reduce costs. Loyalty to one's employees is often a characteristic of a strong leader and the idea of reducing employee numbers or benefits is abhorrent. However, during troubled times, these decisions must be weighed against the success of the company as a whole. If the company fails to survive, *none* of the employees will have salary or benefits; therefore, employee costs must be reviewed as part of a reasonable expense review.

Of course, costs alone cannot drive reductions in this area. In order to ensure that you correctly reduce employee costs you will need to understand not just what every employee costs, but also what each employee does. If your organization is large, this may require the assistance of your management team. From there, review the list to determine if there are any areas in which costs can be reduced. As difficult as it may be to consider, reducing your staff overhead, perhaps by extending your own hours may help you during this initial catch-up period.

The following sections outline areas that you can concentrate on to help you reduce your business costs. If you make the changes to reduce costs in these areas, you will be able to improve your profitability faster.

4.1 Reduce perks

When a company is doing well, small-business owners often pass on some of their success to their employees. Perks such as company phones, cars, extra incentive bonuses, lunches, and other activities may become commonplace. However, when the store is in trouble, these benefits should be reviewed and many should be removed until the company is in a better financial position. The easiest way to explain these reductions to the staff is to let them know that in order to move forward, all perks and bonuses will be based on the company's performance. Further, outline when the bonuses will return. For instance, if the company hits gross sales of "x" then there will be one staff lunch. By providing benefits that are tied to the company profitability instead of simply entitlements, your employees will be motivated to grow the business, not just take advantage of its past successes.

4.2 Reduce benefits

Many companies, when they are profitable, share wealth by offering employees more benefits. However, during difficult markets, occasionally benefits may need to be trimmed to continue to stay competitive.

Health-care plans are an area that you may want to review. Health-care coverage and premiums are constantly changing. Furthermore, regulations around health-care options are also changing dramatically. Reduce your health-care employee expenses by shopping around, comparing benefits and costs.

In some cases, small-business owners may find that it is better for their employees if the company drops their medical plan and switches to a medical reimbursement plan. Although this may sound unusual, for many this will reduce the company's costs and improve the employees' medical options. (For more creative healthcare alternatives for Americans, read *The New Health Insurance Solution*, by Paul Zane Pilzer.)

4.3 Control costs of after-hour meals

If your business regularly reimburses meals to employees who are working late, control costs by organizing evening meals. Ordering off one menu reduces delivery charges, and may encourage a group to share meals (e.g., pizza or subs) to further reduce costs. Also, in order to reduce the costs of individual drinks, keep soda and other refreshments in stock.

4.4 Find a solution for excessive overtime

Overtime can be very expensive for small business owners. Employees paid on an hourly basis are entitled to time-and-a-half for overtime work and sometimes even meal reimbursements. If one or two employees are regularly completing an excessive amount of overtime, it may be cost-effective to add an additional employee part time, rather than pay the additional overtime expenses.

4.5 Deal with weak employees

Some employees may have less to do during a troubled market. As a result, these employees may still be getting paid full-time salaries even though they may no longer be earning them. To resolve this, you may want to consider changing their hours or increasing their workload. Until the volume increases, it may be possible to switch some of these employees to part time during this lull. If possible, you may even want to lay off the weakest performers and add additional new staff members when the company's profitability increases.

4.6 Review employee expenses

In some organizations in which there is little management oversight on employee expenses, employees may take advantage of the system to obtain reimbursements for entertainment and expenses not related to your business. By checking all reimbursements yourself, or at least making a policy of spot-checking reimbursements, you may be able to reduce unnecessary expenses. Remember the responsibility of ensuring that all the expense information is submitted should be part of an employee's responsibility before reimbursements are paid. If you do not have enough information to approve the charges (e.g., a 100-mile gas reimbursement without paperwork documenting the distance to the customer), return the paperwork to the employee and ask for more information.

Lifesaver: If your employees often travel more than 20 miles to your customers, your service may not be as profitable as it may appear. Factoring in mileage reimbursements and hourly employee costs may drop your margin lower than you realize. To counterbalance these expenses, charge your clients a trip fee. This will reduce expenses and may even become a profitable charge for your business.

5. Eliminate Hidden Marketing and Advertising Costs

Marketing and advertising is one of the most critical components to a small business. This could include newspaper and magazine ads, free promotions, public relations, client meals, and any other expense that is designed to draw customers and retain clients. Examples could include free beverages provided to browsing customers, holiday baskets for clients, or promotional giveaways imprinted with the company logo. Each of these items has a cost, but the revenue these items generate should offset these costs. Ideally, your marketing and advertising should bring in more revenue than it costs, but at the very least, you should break even.

Unfortunately, many small-business owners often want to cut their marketing and advertising as soon as times get tight. While this may seem like a good idea because it immediately frees up cash and reduces expenses, it may not be the best course of action for a company that is trying to grow. If you are trying to rebuild a business, you will need to invest your time and sometimes your money in advertising and marketing. Further, the customers you bring in with these tools, presuming they have a positive experience, will also add to your customer base and bring in more customers through referrals.

Instead of simply cutting your advertising, try to reduce the cost of your advertising. Call each marketing company and advertising vendor and ask for a detailed list of your spending. Ask for them to outline each charge and how it applies to your bill. Specifically, ask if there are any additional fees you are paying for specialized and sometimes unnecessary service. You may be surprised at the costs you will find. For example, a newspaper may charge an extra $0.60 per line if any line in the classified ad is bold. Therefore, in order to add one bold line to a small six-line ad, the cost of the ad will increase by $3.60 per day. This means that more than $1,300 per year will be spent on one line of bold in a small classified ad! In this case, unless the bold is a significant advantage it may not be necessary. Ask your advertisers the following questions:

- Is there a difference in cost between a two-color and full-color flyer?

- Does bold print used in the classified ad cost extra?

- Do you provide any discounts if I sign a long-term contract? (Note: Only agree to sign a contract after you are sure that your advertising is bringing in new customers.)

- Am I paying a premium for my location in the periodical?

Aside from understanding your expenses, ask if any additional services are offered with your advertising. For instance some advertisers offer ad design with the purchase of a regular ad spot. They often will help with layout, wordsmithery, color choice, image purchasing, and other design elements in order to retain your business. Using these services instead of outside marketing companies or even in-house staff may save money and even improve your ad's professional appearance.

Another question to ask is whether the advertiser offers any additional advertising opportunities at little or no cost for their regular customers. Some newspaper companies have multiple newspapers in one area. These companies will often display your ad in more than one newspaper for the same price. Although advertising companies may be unwilling to negotiate price, some advertisers may be willing to add additional advertising to retain your business.

Moneymaker: One way to bring in new clients and customers is to become a local expert. To do this you can approach a local small newspaper or magazine (preferably one in which you advertise) and ask if it accepts free articles. Write on topics related to your business and you may be surprised by the amount of traffic it can generate. One magazine we write for brings in at least two new business clients each month.

For each of the promotions that your company provides, ensure that you are including all of the expenses with the promotion. Shipping costs, design costs, and other expenses can make a small promotional giveaway a very large expense. If you are running promotions, make sure that you are leveraging it as much as possible. For instance, if you are giving away an item, it may be valuable to add your custom logo to the product. If you can't afford the logos, a simple, small sticker may be good enough to keep your company name in your customers' minds.

Similarly, if you are spending money on meals and entertainment with your customers, make sure that you are investing your money wisely. In many industries, when times are lucrative, these expenses can grow. Cutting back when times are tight will be understood by your employees and customers alike. In 2000, when the technology sector was booming, and companies were practically throwing money away to build websites, lavish client meals were expected. Today, in a more mild economy, such garish displays in many industries are now considered wasteful and are unnecessary to close a deal.

6. Check Your Own Charges

The last item to review is how much money you, as the owner, take out of the business each month. Consider any expenses you have that you can write off against your business. Meals, entertainment, vehicle expenses, even your salary are expenses that may be able to be reduced so that your business can experience additional growth.

Many small-business owners understand that starting a business is an investment that takes time to build. As one owner of a very successful fire extinguisher business put it, "When we first started, we had very little money. We paid the employees first, the vendors second, the government third, and ourselves last. We didn't take home a paycheck for the first two years." Many owners have similar experiences and if you aren't currently taking a paycheck, you are not alone.

If you are taking a paycheck, you may want to consider reducing your salary. While it is exciting to be able to take money out of the business, it is also important to leave money in the business in order to facilitate growth. Often, expanding takes additional dollars that the business may not have if the owner takes too large a salary. If you are working to expand your business, you will need to leave as much cash in it as possible. In some cases, you may want to look at your home finances and reduce your personal expenses so that you can reduce your salary.

 Lifesaver: As a business owner, you may be entitled to more tax deductions than you would if you simply worked for a business. Reviewing all of your expenses with a tax professional may help identify costs you are paying for out of your pocket that are legitimate business expenses. These items can be paid for by your company and may make it easier to reduce your salary.

7. Do Away with Superfluous Expenses

Doing away with superfluous expenses covers all other business-related expenses. Every other bill, every other credit card charge, and every other cash layout should be included in this category. For most businesses this will include your office supplies, vehicle expenses, staff break room items, cleaning services, magazine subscriptions, organization dues, and other miscellaneous expenses.

The first thing to review is any automated credit card charges. Some charges may be from old expenses that have never properly ended. Check each item and call credit companies to cancel any charges that you cannot identify or no longer need.

Next, review each bill and each item on each bill. These expenses, although sometimes necessary, are usually more elective in nature. Each item should be seriously considered. If possible, the expense should be dropped entirely. For instance, if you are currently paying for cleaning services, consider assigning these tasks to the staff instead of paying an outside agency.

Check your office expenses thoroughly. There are often many opportunities to reduce expenses in this area. For instance, if pens are being ordered, you may want to check what pens and for how much. Paying for expensive office supplies does not necessarily improve the effectiveness of the office. Further, check how often office supplies are being ordered. Does the staff order regularly from a list of approved products? Or are they ordering individual items and paying unnecessary shipping charges? Which products are they choosing? Review your local office store catalog and compare prices. Make sure to include the cost of delivery or mileage if you purchase items in person.

Shipping costs are another type of service that can vary greatly. The cost of shipping the item, the time it takes to get there, and the type of packaging you can use all effect the cost.

Over the last few years, the United States Postal Service has created a very competitive system for packages. With free boxes delivered to your door and low-cost fees, the post office can be a more competitive option for small business shipping.

8. Keep Costs Critical to Expansion

Although cutting bills is important, there are some areas in which you should avoid cutting costs as much as possible. Any item critical to your business success or differentiation should be kept. The following are some examples of items that should not be cut:

- Customer service: Since you are trying to grow your business, you should continue to focus on improving the customer experience, which means maintaining your customer service and not reducing these expenses. Therefore, if your business is known for providing customers free coffee while they wait, reducing this expense could possibly damage customer relationships. Even though this cost may seem unnecessary, the relationship it builds is not worth risking.

- Marketing and advertising: These expenses may be critical to expanding your client base and increasing sales. Any expense in this area should be eliminated only after a thorough review of the cost versus the number of customers and sales is completed. (For more information on tracking the effectiveness of your advertising, see Chapter 8.)

- Insurance: Unfortunately, insurance can never be purchased when you need it most, (e.g., after an accident). Therefore, insurance should not be cut just to reduce a bill.

- Legal and accounting: Although these bills can be some of your most expensive (when counted by the hour) the value of expert legal and accounting advice can often save you more than you pay.

Further, the cost of not consulting a professional can often lead to more unnecessary expenses.

9. Review, Repeat, and Reduce

Once you think you have your complete list of your business expenses, you should continue to review these bills each month to ensure that no billing errors or issues arise. Although most of these items should require no more than a few seconds to review, failing to find errors can be costly. For example, a real estate business found an extra $100 per month was being spent on one rental home's water bill. At first this additional cost was attributed to normal water usage during the hot Arizona summer, but eventually, it was traced to a toilet bowl flapper that had broken two months earlier. Although this repair cost the company only $5 to make, the failure of this trivial part added hundreds of dollars of expense to this company's water bills before the issue was found. If they had continued to ignore monthly bill reviews, the item would have gone unnoticed and the high bill would have continued indefinitely.

4

UNDERSTAND THE FINANCIAL HEALTH OF YOUR ORGANIZATION

Most business owners use accounting systems to monitor their organizations' progress. When you are dealing with an ever-changing market, your financial reports will give you insight into how to respond to economic changes.

By carefully watching the financial health of your organization, you will not only understand your current financial position, but you will be able to notice and take advantage of trends. Perhaps sales increase dramatically on weekends, or products that used to sell well are no longer moving. Maybe repair service has suddenly started to increase. Whatever the change, good or bad, it is important to be aware that each change presents new opportunities. No business can be run on autopilot even if that business is a franchise or other turnkey operation. It will always be necessary to check your market and keep up with trends. Note that even the most popular television commercials

change over time. With each new day you will find new challenges that your business must face and embrace. Therefore, take the time to regularly review all facets of your business.

There are three main reports your business needs to review monthly to understand the financial health of your organization:

- Balance sheet
- Profit and loss statement (also called the P&L statement or the income statement)
- Cash flow statement

Individually, each of these reports provides its own piece of information. However, none of the reports show a complete picture alone. For that you need to review all three reports, for the same dates. The profit and loss statement and the cash flow statement are generally run for a period of time, such as over a month or a quarter. However, the balance sheet is different as it is a "point in time" report. This means that the balance sheet shows a "snapshot" of one point in time.

To get an accurate view of your financials, you should use the last day of the period you chose for your profit and loss statement and the cash flow statement as the day you want to use to run your balance sheet. That will ensure that every charge in the profit and loss statement was taken into account in the balance sheet. For example, you may run one month as follows:

- Profit and loss statement: May 1 through May 31

- Cash flow statement: May 1 through May 31

- Balance sheet: as of May 31

As an entrepreneur, these three reports will help you keep your business on track. Any problems will show on these reports and the advance notice will allow you to make the course corrections necessary to stay competitive.

1. The Balance Sheet

The balance sheet has three parts: assets, liabilities, and owner's equity. It is called a balance sheet because it is usually shown with assets in one section and liabilities and net worth in the other section. Both sections should balance. For example, if your business was to operate entirely in cash, and you withdrew any profits at the end of each period, the balance sheet would be very simple, showing $0 on both sides. However, most businesses don't operate this way. Instead, they have ongoing assets and liabilities. Assets can include product inventory, ownership in buildings, business equipment, cash on hand, and accounts receivable (e.g.,

money owed to the business by customers). Liabilities may include things such as business loans, retained earnings (i.e., profits kept in the business and used to purchase more assets), owner equity, and accounts payable (i.e., money that the business owes others).

From this report, you can track how much money the business currently has on hand (i.e., your current cash position), what assets your business owns (i.e., tools and equipment), and what liabilities are outstanding. Although this report is valuable, alone, it doesn't tell you if the business is making money or losing money. It also won't tell you how much "cash" or money a business is spending each month. For that you will need the next two reports.

2. The Profit and Loss Statement

As mentioned earlier, the profit and loss statement is also known as an income statement or the P&L statement. This statement is usually run each month and shows a list of all the income (profits) and expenses (losses) for the business. This report will only list an item as an "expense" if the payment for the item went to pay a bill. If it paid down principle on a loan, the principle payment for the business will not be included in this report.

At the very bottom of the report is the total of all income and expenses. This number tells you if the business is making a profit or taking a loss. As a business owner, you can use this report to determine if your business is profitable or not. Review these numbers at least once a month to ensure that your business is performing as expected. As soon as you see any slippage, be prepared to start investigating the cause. If the profitability of your business is much less than you were expecting, chances are that your business has a problem that needs to be immediately addressed.

SAMPLE 1
BALANCE SHEET

Assets		Liabilities and Owner's Equity	
Cash	$4,000	Liabilities (loans and accounts payable)	$8,000
Accounts receivable	$5,000	Owner's equity (capital stock and retained earnings)	$11,000
Tools and equipment	$10,000		
Total	**$19,000**	**Total**	**$19,000**

Most accounting programs also allow you to see this report by period (i.e., monthly or quarterly) over the course of a year or even a few years. Therefore, another benefit of this report is that it allows you to look at your business across a few months. From this information, you can see if the company is making more or less money than the previous period. Over time, this trend can tell how fast your business is growing. After you have a year or two of data, you can also identify any seasonal activity.

Now that you have both the profit and loss statement and the balance sheet, you can start to get a more complete financial picture. For instance, from the profit and loss statement it is easy to see that interest was paid; however, it is not possible to see what the current loan amount is. The balance sheet shows the loan amount as of the date of the balance sheet and the profit and loss statement will record that interest on the loan during the period reviewed.

SAMPLE 2
PROFIT AND LOSS STATEMENT

Income	
Sales revenues	$20,000
Cost of goods sold	$10,000
Gross profit on sales	**$10,000**
Expenses	
Rent	$2,000
Payroll	$3,000
Utilities	$1,000
Interest paid	$500
Total operating expenses	**$6,500**
Net Income from Operations	**$3,500**

3. Cash Flow Statement

You need to watch the cash flow statement closely. The cash flow statement tells you how much cash (i.e., real money) comes in and how much goes out each month. It is possible for a business to make money (based on the profit and loss statement) and still have serious cash problems. The cash flow statement will identify if this is an issue for your company. For instance, your profit and loss statement will tell you how much money you make, but paying down loans, such as company vehicles, or purchase loans will not be included as an expense. Therefore, reviewing what your cash position looks like each month will help you prepare for purchases and other cash events.

After you have completed all three statements, they can be read together. In this case, you can see that even though the profit and loss statement says the business is making $3,500 per month, the cash flow analysis shows that there will only be an additional $500 in the cash account at the end of the month. From the cash flow statement, coupled with the profit and lost statement, it is easy to see where the extra $3,000 in "profit" is going:

- $11,000 in inventory purchases on the cash flow statement that were not

SAMPLE 3
CASH FLOW STATEMENT

Cash Inflows (Income)	
Sales and receipts	$20,000
Total cash inflows	**$20,000**
Cash Outflows (Expenses)	
Rent	$2,000
Payroll	$3,000
Utilities	$1,000
Interest paid	$500
Inventory purchases	$11,000
Subtotal of cash outflows (expenses)	**$17,500**
Other Cash Outflows	
Loan principal	$1,000
Owner's draw	$1,000
Subtotal of other cash outflows	**$2,000**
Total Cash Outflows	**$19,500**
Ending Cash Balance	**$500**

included in cost of goods sold on the profit and loss statement

- $1,000 for the loan principle
- $1,000 for the owner's draw

From this, the numbers seem more reasonable. In the last month, inventory has gone up, debt has gone down, and the owner took some money out of the business.

 **Lifesaver:** If you aren't at all familiar with accounting, you are not alone. Many business owners start out with little knowledge in this area. If you need help creating financial statements, or if you want another pair of eyes in interpreting these documents, there are many experts who can help. Your accountant, bookkeeper, or mentor can give you a valuable perspective on these reports.

4. Other Types of Reports to Help You Stay on Top of Your Business

Just because the three financial statements you need are usually produced on a monthly or quarterly basis, doesn't mean that you have to wait to figure out if your business is running off course. There are other reports that you can review on a daily or weekly basis that will allow you to stay on top of your business. If you have an accounting program or point of sale system, chances are these reports are all included.

4.1 Daily and weekly margin report

The margin report should indicate how profitable the business sales actually were. Alone, this report will tell you how much your business makes on a day-to-day basis. If you couple this information with your business's budget, you will be able to see on a daily basis if your business is profitable. To do this, just use your budget and estimate how much your company has to make each day to cover the monthly business expenses. Regularly keeping up with this information will help you guide your day-to-day activities. If you aren't seeing the profitability you were expecting, you can immediately make the course corrections necessary to become more profitable.

4.2 Daily and weekly gross revenue report

The gross revenue report shows the gross sales that the business makes each day. This report will mainly be used to communicate your sales goals to your staff and to determine how well they are doing meeting those goals. Of course, it is not always easy to determine exactly what gross revenue will result in the appropriate margin. Therefore, this report should be reviewed daily at first and compared against the margin report. If your business is meeting the sales goals you have set, your margin should be sufficient to meet the monthly overhead. If your margin is lower than expected, you can immediately adjust the sales goals or make other business changes to prevent a loss for the month.

4.3 Detailed inventory report

If your business requires you to keep inventory, it is important to manage it correctly and track it regularly. If you do not have products available for sale, you risk losing the sale. Depending on how much your company stocks and how quickly the stock runs low, you may need to review your inventory every day, but probably not less frequently than every week.

Of course, a report is only as good as the data in the report. As part of your inventory management, make sure you are doing a full manual inventory at least once every quarter or else these reports could be providing poor or misleading information.

4.4 Customer surveys

Another way to get quick information about what your customers like, dislike, and want is through brief customer surveys. These surveys can be formal, with a customer survey form included at the register, available online, or even as a flyer included with all purchases. Or, they can be informal, conducted by you alone on an as-needed basis. However you choose to do it, getting your customers' candid opinions about your business is an invaluable way to monitor your company.

When you have customers complete a formal survey, you may want to thank them with a discount card. This type of "reward" not only will encourage more people to fill out your surveys, but they will also be more likely to return to your store to make another purchase so that they can use their reward!

5
UNDERSTAND YOUR INDUSTRY TO BECOME A LEADER IN YOUR FIELD

An owner must truly understand the business, the customers, and the industry. For some people, the industry in which they chose to start their business is one they have always enjoyed or one in which they have extensive training For instance, accountants who start their own accounting firms are generally highly skilled in the financial services industry and can be very aware of the fundamentals. However, understanding the details of the industry is not the same as understanding the latest trends in getting customers during tax season.

In order to truly understand the industry, owners need to not just understand one or two products but need to have visibility into what products or services are being offered by competitors, how they are being offered, at what price, and to whom. Without this information, they may have the fundamentals of completing taxes, but lack the ability to get the customers they need to stay in business.

1. Special Note for Franchise Owners

Many franchises will tell you that you don't need to know anything about the franchise industry to run a franchise. Based on the number of successful entrepreneurs who have opened thriving franchises with little or no industry knowledge, industry knowledge is obviously not required. However, that is not to say that it isn't valuable and that it won't help your business grow.

When you speak with customers about the product, or you are looking to invest in a second location or trying to hire the right person for the job, the more information you have the better. Therefore, if you are trying to expand your business or increase your margins, especially on a tight budget, the more knowledge you have the more competitive you can be. Even a franchisee can benefit from industry knowledge and the application of that knowledge.

> **WARNING:**
>
> Before you act on any advice or recommendations from other businesses, make sure that those businesses providing the information are qualified. There are many individuals that tout themselves as small-business experts who have never even owned a business. Advice from these "professionals" can sometimes be misleading or simply incorrect.

2. Learn Your Industry for Free

There are many ways to gain knowledge of how to complete the work for your industry (e.g., trade papers, journals, classes, certifications); however, there are very few that allow you to understand the nuances of your industry. In order to do this, you will probably have to do some searching. The following sections include some of the options you may want to look into.

2.1 Join online chats and newsgroups

Although you may not want to work with competitors in your immediate area, online chats and newsgroups allow you to talk with people in the same industry, but they may be in many different locations. You can share ideas, discuss trends, or consider options without the fear of tipping off the competition. A good place to start looking for groups are free community networking websites such as Yahoo!, LinkedIn, or Facebook.

2.2 Regularly check competitor advertising

If you want to know what your competition is selling, and to whom, pay attention to their advertising. Are they targeting the young professional or the stay-at-home mom? Do they offer free introductory offers or are they more likely to use coupons?

Pay special attention to the advertising of any competitors that are run by major chains. Their ads are usually created by marketing teams that include researchers and trained professionals. By reviewing what they offer and how they offer it you can learn more about what your customer expects. Obviously it would be illegal to run the same or very similar ads, but what you learn from understanding their advertising can be used to improve your own marketing and advertising.

2.3 Visit your competitors

As simple as this sounds, it can be valuable to see exactly what your competition sells and how. If your competition is a large, major chain, you can see how they do business and what they sell without arousing any interest. Watch what the customers request and listen to the salesperson's answers. Take a look at your competitors' product lines. What products do they carry and what don't they stock? Regular trips to visit your competitors will keep you competitive and informed.

2.4 Review your vendor's literature

If your business sells any products, you probably have vendor catalogs from which you order your inventory. Spend time reviewing all the products in the catalog, even if you don't intend to sell them. This review will give you a broad view of what products your customers may be looking for.

Pay special attention to products that you aren't selling but which may be in competition with your product line. Why are your products better? Take the time to compare products side by side so you will be prepared when your customers ask you the very same question.

2.5 Study large competitor websites

One of the best ways to learn more about your industry is through large competitor websites. Big businesses spend millions on building sites that appeal to buyers. Sometimes the features they offer can also help your business. For instance, if you are running a small bookstore, the online business, Amazon, may be a great resource. Amazon has a feature that ranks all books by their popularity. If you are considering expanding your line, this ranking may be a great way to gauge your new products.

2.6 Sign up for industry newsletters and magazines

Many companies provide their customers and others with free industry newsletters that track trends in their industry. Signing up for these free mailers is a great way to keep up with your competition and stay informed on the latest trends. A good place to find these opportunities is on your competitors' websites. Just be careful which email address you use. Ideally, don't use any address that immediately reveals that you are a competitor.

Some industries (e.g., technology) have free industry magazines to which you can subscribe. The easiest way to find these magazines is through online searches. Make sure to include your industry in your search terms.

2.7 Take free training courses

Sometimes, vendors will offer free training courses to increase your knowledge about their products and its place in the industry. Taking advantage of these courses is a great way to learn more and to network with other players in your industry. To find out if any of your vendors offer these classes, check their websites regularly or speak with your sales agent.

Lifesaver: Creating a "free information" rack that displays useful brochures for your customers is a great way to share your industry knowledge with your patrons. One local pediatrician's office has about 20 different pamphlets on topics ranging from vaccines to puberty. Having these pamphlets lets parents get more information, reduces questions to staff, and lends authority to the doctor's office.

3. Investing in Your Education

There are times when you may want to rely on formal programs instead of free materials. Typically, this is most important when your business requires specialized knowledge or skills. In some cases, customers will expect either you or your employees to be formally trained in these functions before they will do business with you. Usually, the larger the business of the clients, the more likely they will want formal training in the staff of the businesses they deal with.

3.1 Complete certifications

In some industries, an immediate way to gain consumer confidence is with the completion of industry-recognized certifications. Before you invest in the cost of the test, which can be expensive, make sure you have all the required study material. Sometimes, special books, or even training courses are the fastest, easiest, and least expensive ways to complete these tests.

After your employees complete their certifications, add the certification logo or term to the employees' business cards so that your customers are aware that your business has this expertise.

3.2 Online courses

Some colleges or companies offer online classes that allow you to gain formal training in a business technology or skill. Through online classes, you and your employees can take every course from a brief introductory overview of a topic to a Masters of Business Administration (MBA). Depending on what your customers expect, these courses may be valuable.

3.3 Group membership

In almost any industry there seem to be exclusive groups that require members to meet certain requirements before they join. Sometimes these requirements are as simple as paying a fee and maintaining yourself in good standing; other times, these groups are more stringent. Joining these groups can sometimes be very valuable. Just make sure that when you spend the money to get a membership that you prominently display the group logo throughout your business and on your website. There is no point in maintaining a membership that your customers are not aware of.

3.4 Read the latest industry-related books

Regularly review the new books that come out in your industry. Sometimes, these books will be pivotal in the industry and will be important conversation pieces with your customers. In some cases, you can even use these books to support your product sales and validate your business. Also, understanding what the latest research implies for your business is an important part of staying current in your industry.

4. Spread the Knowledge

Once you determine the best ways to gain knowledge in your industry, encourage your employees to do the same. The following list includes some ways to encourage your team to learn more about the industry:

- Offer "lunch and learn" sessions: Ask the team to bring their lunch (or provide lunch for the group) while one person discusses a new industry trend or product.

- Reimburse employees for training or certifications: If training or certification will result in additional sales for your business, you may want to consider reimbursing employees for completing training courses or certification exams.

- Distribute appropriate articles and information: If you find a particular article, book, or newsletter valuable, take the time to distribute it to your team and discuss it with them. To ensure it adds value, make sure to highlight a few of the key points you want them to learn.

Remember: Knowledge, if used correctly, can help your employees educate your customers, which can result in more sales for your business!

6
ASK FOR SUPPORT AND ASSISTANCE

Some business owners choose to run their business alone. However, that puts the entire pressure of the business on one person — all decisions, problems, and complaints must be solved by the owner alone. Employees may be able to assist, but since most employees haven't owned their own business, too often, these individuals cannot provide the answers the business needs.

When an owner enlists support, it is possible to learn from the mistakes and successes of others without having to experience each decision. For a business owner, the value of this experience is significant. Businesses with a strong support system are able to grow faster and more confidently than others in the same environment. When we started enlisting support from other business owners, family, and friends, we found a wealth of valuable information, ideas, and guidance readily available.

No matter where you are, what your business does, or whom you know, there are many ways for a small business owner to find support and assistance. It is never necessary to face all of the challenges of turning a business around alone.

1. Ask for Help

Owning a business can be a very personal experience. Most owners put their heart, soul, and money into a business and therefore are vested in the outcome of the company. For many people, the cost of failure is bankruptcy and then the difficulty involved in starting over. After all, a true entrepreneur finds it nearly impossible to give up on owning his or her own business. To most business owners, the idea of simply returning to the rat race and a regular, lackluster nine-to-five job as an employee is not appealing and is not a real option. Therefore, the only thing for a dedicated owner to do is to identify the problem, and solve it as quickly as possible. How it is solved and by whom has to be secondary to the success and financial growth of the business.

If it doesn't matter where a solution comes from, why not take all the assistance and guidance possible? Seek out the best individuals possible to solve the problem. Sometimes this will mean engaging professionals such as accountants, lawyers, and other specialists, but also, this may mean finding help from less traditional sources.

Don't be afraid to recruit your own family or closest friends to help you succeed. Some of these people may have already offered to help. Take advantage of this help if you can. When your business is facing challenges, you will need even more time to commit to making the changes your business needs to be successful. Recruiting assistance from your spouse, children, parents, or close friends will allow you to delegate some tasks to trustworthy individuals. Don't worry that you may not be able to pay them back immediately; you can always repay them when your business is rich and successful. After all, chances are they feel as invested in its success as you do.

Once you start engaging others in your business decisions, you may find yourself getting some ideas and suggestions that you immediately want to implement. When we started working more with people, we were able to immediately implement some great ideas. Of course, some were more candid than we expected. When we sent photos of the store to a close family member, she took one look and immediately said, "Wow! Your store sure is messy." While this wasn't the response we were expecting (or really even wanted), it did identify a problem that no employee or customer had been candid enough to bring up. We realized we had to clean things up and get them organized. Based on that one comment, we completely redesigned the store. We knew she was correct when our regular customers continually complimented us on the new layout.

This does not mean that you will want to take all the ideas you receive. Sometimes advice will seem obviously incorrect, but other times, you will have to use your own judgment. Even experts and consultants can have their own bias on how to run a business, which may not work for your company. As the business owner you will need to learn when to take suggestions and when to diplomatically turn them down. In the end, the responsibility for the business will still be yours so make sure you can justify any suggestion you take. Don't let well-meaning advice misdirect your company.

Lifesaver: Hiring family members to work in your business can be an economical way to get more done for less. Family members care about the long-term success of the business and may be willing to make financial sacrifices to give the business the chance to become successful. Unlike most employees, family members may be willing to accept lower salaries or even defer their salaries altogether during a cash-flow crisis.

2. Get Support from Your Spouse

Any small-business owner in a committed relationship will tell you a business can put a strain on a relationship, especially if that business is struggling to grow and compete. However, it doesn't have to. One way to help alleviate this potential strain is to share some of the business burden with your spouse or significant other. Some couples actually find that owning a business together is a great opportunity to share time and work together toward a common goal.

Let your spouse know what is going on in the business and what challenges you face. This simple act of talking through your opportunities and ideas will help solidify your plans and may even result in additional ideas from your spouse. For example, a friend of ours was considering opening a small computer store in a nearby town. He asked his wife as well as us if we would like to see his new planned location. The storefront was in a busy shopping center and there was little competition in the immediate neighborhood. It seemed like a good location. After he finished showing us around, his wife, who up until then had been very quiet, asked a simple question, "Is this town really big enough for a computer store?" The question caught us all by surprise. The town was less than 30 minutes outside Phoenix, but it was geographically isolated. After we ran the demographics around our store, and compared the two towns, we realized that she was correct; the town might not be large enough to support a computer store easily. Since then, another computer store opened in that area and in less than one year it closed.

By including your spouse in your business you may find that his or her unique perspective brings new ideas or improvements that you hadn't considered before. Even if your spouse is unfamiliar with your industry, technology, products, or running a business in general, his or her enthusiasm and support can be invaluable.

Moneymaker: Leverage your family and friends whenever possible as your unpaid sales force. Make sure they always have a few of your company's business cards or brochures handy. To make their "sales pitch" more legitimate, create special discount cards that they can distribute as a "friends and family discount." This will allow them to refer their friends and associates even more easily.

3. Take Your Children to Work

If your children are school age, you may want to include them in the business as well. Since you are the business owner, your children can work for the business before they could normally work at an outside job. Plus, having them help around the store or office will allow you to delegate simple, small, time-consuming tasks and free you for other activities. High-school children can run the register, complete inventories, make store signs, and even learn some basic bookkeeping. For younger children, stacking shelves, emptying trash cans, and cleaning windows may be helpful. Having your children involved will also give you more time with them, which is always valuable.

If you choose to have your children help you in your store or office, you may pay them a salary that is comparable to what you would pay an employee to complete the same tasks. This will allow you to take advantage of the child's lower tax rate. However, you should always contact a qualified tax accountant before implementing any tax strategies.

4. Get Advice from the Experts

While advice from those closest to you can be great, it is even better when you can have guidance from experienced experts. Having a mentor can often make the difficult job of running a business easier. Mentors are seasoned individuals that can guide you through the daily challenges you will face and can provide experienced answers to your toughest questions. Most often, mentors will take this challenge because they enjoy helping others grow into their new business.

Many of the best mentors we have found have offered their advice for free. The largest cost to the business owner is often just taking his or her mentor out for coffee or lunch. Usually mentors simply want to get involved because they enjoy the challenge of growing a business and teaching a new entrepreneur the ropes.

Another benefit is that seasoned businesspeople who become mentors often have a network of business partners in accounting, law, bookkeeping, banking, insurance, and other industries that they can recommend. Having an arsenal of seasoned references is very useful whether your business is in trouble or doing well. During the rough times, these professionals can be looked to for guidance on negotiating debts, getting money, or even handling difficult financial situations. When your business starts to take off, these same people will help you make the right tax decisions, finance the right expansion projects, and build a stronger financial foundation for your business.

To find a good mentor, look for someone who has already retired from running one or more small businesses. These experienced entrepreneurs have often sold their own business and now are "retired" into boredom. Often these retired business owners will be willing to help small-business owners.

WARNING:

Beware of experts who claim to be able to perform miracles with business development. Companies that sell advertising, business leads, or consulting services do not usually guarantee their results. While some of these professional services may be worthwhile, always get referrals and ask for references before you purchase any "expert" advice.

Once you find a mentor, you both may need to decide if you are compatible. While it is great to find a mentor who may be in your industry or line of business, it is even more important to find a mentor who shares your values and understands your goals and objectives for the business. Taking the time to talk with potential mentors about the long-term vision of your company and your current business challenges will let you determine if the match will be beneficial.

There are many ways to find a mentor in your area who will be willing to work with you to grow your business. The following sections will help you get started.

4.1 SCORE — Counselors to America's Small Business

SCORE is a nonprofit organization that focuses on educating entrepreneurs in the US. This education can take many forms. There are business tips, conferences, financial templates, question and answer areas, technology recommendations, and even financing options. It is a valuable resource no matter your location or industry.

SCORE volunteers include working and retired executives, corporate leaders, and business owners who act as business counselors to entrepreneurs. The volunteers work with entrepreneurs to help start, grow, and develop their companies.

To attend a meeting, find a local mentor or speak to someone directly, you can check the SCORE website to find your closest chapter (www.score.org). You can usually arrange a meeting with one or more of the volunteers. These business-savvy individuals can help you with most aspects of running your business — from your original business plan to troubleshooting individual issues. If there is no local chapter in your area, you should review the website to find a way to identify a mentor in your area.

4.2 US Small Business Administration (SBA)

The US Small Business Administration is a not-for-profit government organization that specializes in assisting small-business owners. On the SBA website (www.sba.gov) you will find free training, small-business tools, and other great resources for small businesses.

4.3 Resources for Canadian businesses

Industry Canada offers information on many business topics. It also provides links to other sites that offer mentoring for business entrepreneurs. Visit www.ic.gc.ca.

If you are between the ages of 18 and 34, you may want to consider contacting the Canadian Youth Business Foundation (CYBF). They hand-match each entrepreneur with a business mentor. For more information go to www.cybf.ca.

5. Develop Relationships with Other Business Owners

By developing relationships with other business owners, you can find people who are facing the same challenges you are. Even if these individuals have not been in business long, talking and meeting regularly is a great way to brainstorm new ideas, exchange helpful tips, and get practical feedback. Set up network meetings so that you can help each other and become familiar with each other's products. By sending customers to your business network, and them sending customers to you, you will all profit with new sales opportunities.

Another benefit is that other small-business owners may be interested in partnering on advertising, which is one of the largest expenses for many businesses. One printing company we know partners with other small businesses and sends out a mailer once a month. This mailer is inexpensive for them to produce and by working with other small-business owners everyone benefits. The printing company gets their advertising and their business partners pay less than they would have to send out a mailer alone. This type of cooperative advertising helps save money and increases sales.

There are many different ways to get to know other business owners in your area. One way to find local business owners is to get to know your customers. You may be surprised to learn that many of your customers may be small-business owners as well. Try to find other business owners in similar circumstances. If you are in a strip mall, there are probably other business owners nearby that are looking to grow and expand their businesses. Working together, you may be able to share successful advertising in your area, split postcard costs, or share customer lists. These relationships will also allow you to understand your area as you discuss the business trends and growth patterns.

Moneymaker: Getting to know your neighbors can be an easy way to gain new customers. If your business is in a strip mall or office complex, other stores can be a great source of referrals and leads. Just arrange to leave a freestanding brochure holder or business card holder with a few brochures, flyers, or cards in each neighborhood store. This low-cost advertising is an easy way to bring in new local customers.

---

6. Get Advice from Your Franchise Company

If you are a franchisee, very often your franchise company can help you through a difficult time. Odds are that your franchise fee already includes marketing materials and some advertising support. Contact your parent company for more ideas on what you can do to bring in new customers.

If you are looking to meet peers, you may also want to try meeting other owners in the franchise. You can then start your own support group to share ideas and improve your businesses.

7
TAKE STOCK OF YOUR SUPPLIES

In a tough economy, the amount of money available to spend decreases. People become much more careful about where they spend their money. Things formerly considered vital become discretionary. Whereas in past years customers might have been willing to pay more for quality goods and services, when money is tight, customers want more for less. Therefore, although it may sound simplistic, one of the best ways for a business to provide this value is by reducing how much they spend on inventory and expenses. If you pay less, you can charge less, while keeping your margins intact and retaining customers. Reducing your product and service costs whenever possible can have a significant positive impact on your company's bottom line.

1. Reducing Inventory Costs

Typically, there are two parts to the cost of inventory, the cost of the product itself and the cost of shipping the product. However, there are other, subtle expenses associated with inventory purchases. There is the time the employees spend making the order, the time that it takes to receive and unpack the shipment, as well as the time it takes to put the inventory on the shelves. Companies that have inventory can sometimes use the following ways to reduce their costs dramatically:

- Order larger quantities: Some companies provide volume discounts on products. If your business has storage capacity, this can reduce product costs. Usually you pay less for items and you don't waste employee time reordering or checking in multiple orders.

- Check shipping costs: Sometimes the low-cost vendor is not the one with the lowest shipping and handling charges. Make sure when you are comparing prices of vendors you include the cost of shipping.

- Change suppliers: Regularly check different suppliers to see if you can purchase any of your products at lower costs.

- Purchase from discount retailers: Sometimes local large warehouse stores (e.g., Sam's Club or Costco) can be a less expensive alternative for product sources. Occasionally, special sale prices may make it less expensive to order a product from a retailer than it is to get it from a regular supplier.

Moneymaker: Whenever you purchase products for resale make sure to present your reseller certification. This document shows that your business is a legitimate reseller. Purchases your business makes to sell to your customers will therefore be free of sales tax. Even retailers (as opposed to wholesalers) will honor this documentation. Most will even let you keep this document on file with them to make future purchases faster and easier.

- Reduce unnecessary variety: If your store typically sells two or three products, but carries 17 different types, you may want to reduce this variety as it adds unnecessary management overhead and can cause confusion when you are trying to sell any of these products.

- Purchase products together when possible: In some cases, components may be more expensive than product groups that are being pushed by suppliers. For instance, in the computer industry some suppliers actually charge significantly more for a computer case, mouse, and keyboard purchased individually than they do when you purchase these three items as a group.

- Return damaged goods quickly: When you receive orders, you may find that some items are not in working condition. Return these items as soon as possible for either a refund or new product.

- Track vendor quality: Many companies will make you pay your own shipping on returns, so the cost of damaged goods can be expensive. Keep a record of vendors' and manufacturers' quality levels and review regularly. You may need to switch companies if damaged products increase your overhead too significantly.

2. Stock Products, Not Catalogs

While this may seem obvious, some store owners try to encourage catalog shopping for their patrons. Instead of having products available, these owners will have the catalogs there to show the patrons what type of products they can get. While this has its benefits — inventory costs remain low since there is no chance of ordering a product that doesn't sell and you can offer a wide range of products — it is not always the best way to go. Many people will be reluctant to purchase a product they haven't seen. After all, if they were comfortable with catalog shopping, they probably would have made their purchases online instead of coming into a retail store.

The best time to use catalogs is when your customer wants an upgraded or downgraded version of a product that you already display and sell. In this case, the customer has already seen the product and instead wants something slightly different. By allowing customers to make choices, it is possible to have the best of both worlds. You can keep your inventory costs down by carrying the most popular products and then continue to make sales by offering more customized products.

3. Get Rid of Old Products

Some businesses are full of old products that haven't sold in years. Unfortunately, these products take up space and worse yet, may be a turnoff to some customers. If products have been in inventory too long, it may be necessary to get rid of some of the old, unpopular stock. There are many ways to free up this space while recovering most of the money that was invested in the products:

- Donations: Choosing to donate any unpopular products to a tax deductible charity may not immediately recover the product costs, but when tax time approaches, the cost of the goods may be tax deductible. Always speak to a qualified accountant before choosing to donate anything to determine exactly how much of the cost of the products can be written off.

- Discounting: Selling unwanted products at a steep discount or even at cost can recover the product investment as well as generate some excitement from your customers.

- Auction sites: Even if the customers in your immediate area aren't interested in the products, it is still possible that other individuals will want to purchase your products. Put the items on eBay or another auction site.

- Freebies: If you want to build customer loyalty more than recover product costs, give away your unwanted products. Each time your customers make a significant purchase, provide a choice of products. In some businesses you can use these items as an incentive or reward to close the sale.

Even if you don't get your full investment back, removing this old stock from your inventory will open up your store, and allow you to make room for new, profitable merchandise.

4. Reducing Assembled Product Costs

When you are reviewing your expenses, you also should review how much the assembly of your products actually costs your business. If your business currently assembles any products, there is a cost associated with that assembly — even if you, the owner, complete the assembly yourself. If building your product causes you to be unable to complete any other task (e.g., selling to customers or growing revenues), then the assembly is costly and you may be able to save money by outsourcing to another vendor. Of course, before you make this decision, you need to add up each cost associated with building the product.

WARNING:

In some industries, it may be more profitable to have onsite assembly even when it is less expensive to purchase premade products. Many restaurants are well known for their "homemade" foods and desserts. In this case, even though the cost of the product may be more expensive, the customer experience is significantly better. This difference can result in more referrals and purchases, which means that the more expensive "homemade" product may actually be more profitable.

When we assembled our products at our store we were shocked by the results. Like many businesses, we build our own products (i.e., computers) because we want to sell our customers only the best, most reliable product available. However, it was always assumed that assembling these products ourselves would be less expensive than ordering the products and having the supplier assemble them. What we found was just the opposite was true.

Because the technicians were assembling the computers, at various times throughout the day our company was experiencing unnecessary problems and unnecessary costs. The ten or more components were difficult for the technicians to track, especially with their other repair work. Parts that were used in assembly were often found to be damaged, incurring an additional cost to return them to the vendor. Also, because the actual assembly could be time consuming, there were times when there were no new computers for sale in the store. When we researched alternatives, we found that for a small fee, our product vendor would allow us to choose the components ourselves (to ensure they met our high quality standards) and then assemble them, test them, and ship the completed machines to our store. It saved a significant amount of money, increased sales on new machines, reduced our inventory management issues, simplified ordering, and freed up technicians to handle repairs.

To determine if it is possible to outsource your product assembly, you need to start by adding up all the costs included in putting the item together. Include any task that is completed by you or your staff and as well as the cost of any items that you use during assembly. The following list outlines what should be included in your calculations of the cost:

- Cost of each component: Make sure to include both the cost of the component and any shipping costs on each item.

- If you or your employees are completing the assembly, the cost of assembly is not just the time to put the product together. Make sure to include estimates for the following:
  - Tracking inventory: If your product takes multiple parts to assemble, chances are you spend time making sure those parts are in stock.
  - Ordering components: Every product you order adds complexity to the ordering system.
  - Receiving purchases: Include the time it takes to receive the purchases, add the components into inventory, and store them away for later assembly.
  - Assembling the new product: Include the time to collect all the components as well as the time it takes to assemble the product.
  - Repackaging the new product (if necessary).
  - "Inventorying" the new product: Include the time to take the parts out of inventory and add the new product back into inventory.

Once you have the total time for all of these tasks, you can determine the total cost by multiplying the time by the cost of your labor. Remember, this labor cost should be the "loaded" cost for the employee including all the costs such as salary, payroll tax, and benefits.

- Management overhead: Whenever a complex task such as product assembly is completed, it needs to be managed. Each task above usually has a management component, which should be included.

- Disposable goods: If your business uses paper forms or other disposable goods during assembly, include these costs as well.
- Cost of damaged components: If you are assembling components to build your product, there will be a cost to repair or return parts that are not in working order.

Once you think you understand the full cost of assembling your products, start shopping around for other vendors. Do not be afraid to call overseas manufacturers, local businesses, and local distributors. You may be surprised by how competitive the prices are. Companies that perform assemblies for many different distributors can usually reduce the overhead of assembly more than any small vendor. If possible, take advantage of this to reduce your costs, and free up your employees for more profitable tasks.

> # WARNING:
> Before choosing to purchase preassembled products, make sure that the company doing the work has both a product test procedure and a strong guarantee for their workmanship. Only do business with companies that have high quality standards. Otherwise, the high cost of handling dissatisfied customers and trying to return damaged products can quickly eliminate any money saved by purchasing premade goods.

After you have the real cost of assembling your products, you should regularly (at least once a year), sit down and review the assembly costs to determine if anything changed.

Your costs could have risen, or the cost to assemble the product may have gone up (especially if you are working offshore and dealing with varying currencies). Depending on the amount you pay your employees, the costs of parts and the time it takes to build, you may not want to change how you assemble your product.

5. Reducing Service Costs

Unfortunately, most of the cost of completing a service for a customer is the cost of the employees providing that service. However, there are still opportunities to reduce this overhead:

- Consider offshoring: If your business has any service components that do not need to be completed on-site, you may be able to outsource this work offshore and pay significantly reduced rates. You can generally offshore anything from bookkeeping to customer service.
- Hire junior-level employees: If your business has tasks that can be completed by less experienced personnel, it may be possible to hire less experienced individuals for these tasks and free up the more senior and expensive individuals for higher paid services.

Moneymaker: Interns can be a great way to get enthusiastic, low-cost employees. As an alternative to pay, call local high schools and colleges and work with their placement office to find ways to offer young employees course credit for their time. Depending on how you structure your intern program you may be able to pay the intern nothing in exchange for the experience and training.

6. Revenue Does Not Equal Profit

When people ask a business owner how much money his or her business makes per year, the answer is usually the gross revenue of the business. This means the total amount the company brings in from customer receipts. As a result, many employees and even customers are familiar with this number. What they do not know is what expenses the business has. After all, a business can have millions in gross revenue, but if the expenses are higher than they should be, the business can actually be losing money. Revenue has absolutely no relationship to profit. For instance, the cost of a meal at a restaurant is not based on just the cost of the food, or even the cost of the chef or food servers to prepare and serve the food. The true cost of the meal includes everything from the rent of the building to the cost of getting the linens cleaned. Unfortunately, not everyone understands the true costs of doing business.

7. Your Products and Services Cost

One of the more common misperceptions employees have is that a business owner is making a profit of 80 to 90 percent on services and products that are sold. This is because it is very easy for employees, customers, and sometimes even business owners to underestimate the cost of products or services. Even after adding up all the costs that go into buying inventory or providing a service, many people still forget that a business has other overhead as well. Employees will make assumptions about the cost of doing business that are just not correct. This type of complaint happens frequently. When employees are unhappy, customers can tell, and your business can be negatively impacted.

One hairstylist we know once lamented that his boss made "too much money." He argued that the company was getting paid significantly more for a haircut than he was taking home, and he did all the work! As business owners, we know this type of simple math is obviously incorrect. The salon owner has not just the salary of the hairstylist, but the payroll taxes, the overhead to maintain the storefront, advertising and marketing costs, and probably much more. What seems like a simple calculation at first is much more difficult to calculate than most people realize.

Unfortunately, this type of misperception is common and it is your responsibility to keep morale solid. That is not to say that as a business owner you should outline to your customers every cost and bill you pay; however, you should not be embarrassed to make a profit on the products and services you offer.

Helping employees understand the full costs of your products and services will help them sell with confidence. If they believe you are "ripping off" the customers, they will project that and your sales will plummet. Another benefit of being transparent with your employees is that when they understand the costs they may even be able to volunteer ways to save your business money.

8
FOCUS ON YOUR TARGET MARKET

If you want your business to be successful, you must identify what you want to sell, to whom you want to sell, and how your products and services differ from your competitors'. Failing to do this will waste your precious resources on advertising campaigns that don't work.

When you first opened your business, you probably had an idea of what type of company you were trying to create. You knew exactly what you would sell and to whom. However, choosing the direction of your business is not a one-time exercise. A business needs to constantly review its direction to ensure that it remains on course. What marketing campaign can be effective without a target?

Therefore, if you want to effectively market your business, you must know who your customers are today, not yesterday.

1. Products That Appeal to Everyone

Some businesses feel that they have products that are so widely used and so well known that these items appeal to everyone. If you believe that your products or services fall into this "mass appeal" category, you may be misleading yourself and your business. The truth is that no product appeals to everyone. To labor under the false belief that something can be used by everyone can waste both time and money that most businesses don't have.

Take retail clothing as an example. A retail clothing store could sell to women of any age, and any walk of life, but in truth, they rarely do. Think of a specific women's retail clothing store that is local to your area. The moment you walk in the store, you forge an impression that determines whether or not you want to shop there. The price of the clothes lets you know who can afford to shop there. The size and the style of the clothes limit the customers further. It would be impossible for any clothing store to carry all styles, sizes, and price ranges, so no store tries to sell to every woman. Instead, clothing stores tend to focus on their main consumer and try to appeal to that demographic. This successful strategy then allows them to customize their product line even further, build appropriate accessory lines, target advertising, and much more. Without this information, a store wouldn't know what to buy, sell, or display.

One thing the business owners with whom we spoke have in common is that they easily articulate what demographic represents the majority of their customers. Having this focus allows them to drive their advertising and marketing, add new products to their product lines, and expand their businesses with confidence. They know what their customers want and can therefore grow faster and more profitably than the average business. Further, when they want to expand by opening a second location or branch into a new market, they know exactly what type of group they are looking for and how they will target customers in the new area. Focus and customer knowledge make this type of growth possible. It can help lower the business owner's risk and increase the chances of success in a new venture.

2. Identify Your Target Market

Take a moment to document whom you think your customers are. Be as specific as possible. For instance, think back to the retail clothing example in section **1**. While it might be technically accurate to say that the customers are typically women, this is not specific enough. When you try to identify your customers, try to identify as many characteristics to describe them as

possible. A better example may be to say that the customers are typically women between the ages of 15 and 25 who live within ten miles of the business, and regularly purchase stylish, low-cost clothing. The following are some examples of customer characteristics that you can use to identify your business's target market:

- Customer location: Where are your customers typically found? The customer's location does not just mean a home address; for instance, a restaurant may find its lunch customers typically work within five miles of the business, but that doesn't mean that the customers live within five miles. Categorize your customers by zip or postal code, city, county, or state or province. The more specific you can be the better.

- Gender: If most of your customers are women or men (i.e., 70 percent or more), you can use gender as a characteristic; however, for many businesses gender may not be relevant.

- Age: The age of your customers may or may not be relevant. If you're selling false teeth, perhaps, but if you're selling groceries, probably less so.

- Income level: Whether your business caters to other businesses or to individuals, the income of your customers or clients can matter significantly. For example, high-end jewelry stores will not be selling to low-income customers.

- Knowledge: To understand the knowledge level of your customers, try to document how much information your customers have about the product or service. Identify if your typical customers are very knowledgeable or if they require your company's support.

- Homeowner or renter: In some businesses, customers being homeowners is very critical. For instance, plumbers, painters, and other home-service companies will find this category very important.

Depending on your business, this list may vary. Each business has its own customer characteristics. Be sure to include any other data that may be important to your business.

Business-to-business companies may find their categories varying dramatically from this. For example, our business customers are typically small business owners who make less than $5 million gross, have a business office or store within ten miles of our storefront, and currently have fewer than ten employees.

Once you are comfortable with how you documented who you *think* your customers are, it is necessary to then find out who they really are.

Moneymaker: Including advertising in with customer purchases or invoices can be an easy, low-cost way to increase sales. A simple flyer that offers a discount for return customers or advertises new products can cost less than a few pennies a page and can result in new sales. For more targeted results, make a few different inserts with suggestions that complement the customer's last purchase.

---

3. Discover Who Your Customers *Really* Are

Determining who your customers are can be more difficult than it first seems. Unfortunately, it is not as simple as observing who comes into your store and buys your products. For instance, let's say a woman in her mid-30s walks into your store and purchases your most popular product. You cannot simply assume that your typical customers are women in their mid-30s. You still need to know what makes her your customer demographic. Seeing her purchase the product doesn't tell you much about her. You don't know where she lives, what she typically earns, or even if she is purchasing your product for herself or as a gift. If you only have very general information about your customers, you probably don't have enough information to find and advertise to more customers like her.

For example, if you have a children's clothing store, that woman may be a customer because she is a mother of three children younger than the age of five. If your typical customer falls within this demographic, you may find that expanding your line to include small inexpensive toys may bring in new revenue since many women make small impulse purchases for their children. However, what if she isn't a mother and instead is a single woman who just bought a baby shower gift for a coworker? If this is your typical customer, then you may want to add a few gift cards, gift baskets, and bows to your product line.

Depending on what type of customer you typically have, your decisions will need to be different. In the last two examples the customer's age and gender are not as important as it first appeared. This initial, superficial observation is valuable, but it is not enough information to create a targeted marketing campaign or to customize your business.

Unfortunately, the task of identifying who your customers are, what they purchase, and why is a complicated task that is the focus of many books, articles, and expert advice. In general, this is one of the most intricate aspects of running a business. When you start studying this topic, you will find that it can consume almost any amount of time that you have. Yet, as a business owner, it is necessary to get to the basics of this information as quickly and inexpensively as possible. Therefore, instead of focusing on the details and nuances, start out at a higher level and work your way into the details later.

3.1 Learn about your customers

It would be great if you could have your customers complete a brief profile every time they came into your store. Some large retailers do just that, tracking their customers by loyalty cards and private credit cards. With this information, they can pull the customer's address and use data mining techniques to make generalizations. They can derive typical customer income levels, education levels, and even values. If you don't have money for this type of extravagant service, it is still possible to learn a great deal about your customers without investing a dime.

The simplest, least expensive, and most accurate way to gather customer information is to talk to them and ask them questions. Pay attention to how they interact with you and your staff. Watch how they browse in your store. Find out if they usually ask for help or if they know what they want as soon as they come into the store. During the sales process (preferably after they have committed to the sale) try to engage them in small talk. Some questions you can ask your customers include:

- Can I have your address to add to our mailing list?

- Would you like a gift receipt for that? (If it is a gift, go on to ask whom the gift is for.)

- How did you hear about us?

- Did you find everything you needed?

- Did anyone help you with this purchase?

When a customer gives you this information, make sure to record as much detail as you can. Any information you gather can be used to ensure that you are meeting your customer's expectations. Start to categorize the data, when possible, using the same categories you used to identify your expected customer groups. Just make sure you and your employees ask all purchasing customers for this information.

When you decide to start this type of survey, make sure to stress to your employees the importance of asking for this information from all your customers and show your employees how to record the information accurately. Do not expect all your customers to answer. Some may choose not to answer any questions about themselves, while others will be overly forthcoming. This is fine for the statistics you want to capture. However, if you or your employees only ask some customers for this information (and not all) your data will be incomplete. Since you no longer have a survey of all customers, your results will not represent your customer base and you may draw erroneous conclusions from this misleading data.

Lifesaver: If you use an electronic point-of-sale system, this program may allow you to add custom fields for every customer. Saving this information directly in your system will make it easier to find this data later and manage reporting. If your system doesn't have this functionality, or if you don't use a point-of-sale system, a simple customer list (preferably on an electronic spreadsheet) will work almost as well.

Gathering answers to various questions is the first step to understanding your customers, but until you transform this data into easy-to-read tables, you will probably not be able to get any actual information from what you collected. As many owners have learned, there is a big difference between data and information. The statistics you have collected such as customer information, purchases, and margins is still just "data." In this current form, it is not possible to tell much from the answers to your questions. The next step is to combine the data in such a way that it tells who your customers are, what they like, what they buy, and what advertising works best. That is when the data becomes useful information. After you have been gathering the data for a week or more, you probably have enough to get started.

3.2 Discover your customer demographics

Discover your customer demographics by creating a few categories for your customers (use the category types mentioned in section **2.**. Make sure that you only group your data by the level of specificity you actually have. For instance, if you haven't asked each customer for his or her birthday, you probably have no more than a general idea of your customer's ages. Therefore, do not try to be too specific when you are grouping by age. However, if you own a liquor store and keep track of the birthdays of your customers (to make sure they are older than 21), you may be able to get very specific in the age category. For the average business though, a typical customer-tracking grid may look like Table 1.

Table 1 shows a very small group of customers — in the entire table only 50 customers are represented. Although this is a very small sample size, it is still enough to begin to notice patterns and start identifying the customer demographic for this store. Some data you can see from this simple table includes:

- Customer age group: The vast majority of customers for this business (i.e., 42 customers or 84 percent of all customers) are between the ages of 18 and 50. If you wanted, you could try to break down this category further to determine if the age range was evenly distributed between everyone from 18 to 50 or did most of your customers fall between the 25 to 35 age range.

- Customer location: Most customers for this business (i.e., 40 customers or 80 percent) come from only two zip/postal

TABLE 1
CUSTOMER-TRACKING GRID INCLUDING AGE AND ZIP/POSTAL CODE

	18 – 30	31 – 50	51+	Total by Zip/Postal Code
Zip/Postal Code 1	I	I		2
Zip/Postal Code 2	IIII II	IIII II	III	17
Zip/Postal Code 3	IIII IIII	IIII III	IIII	23
Zip/Postal Code 4	III	II		5
Zip/Postal Code 5	I	II		3
Total by Age	**22**	**20**	**8**	**50**

codes. In general, you would expect these two zip/postal codes to fall very close to your business.

Once you know the zip or postal code where most of your customers live, you can use free online tools to gather additional general information about the customers. There are many sites in the US that provide this information for free (e.g., Zipskinny.com). For each category, these websites don't just show median values, but usually show the breakdown as a percentage of the population including:

- Household income level
- Education achievement level
- Marital status
- Occupations
- Racial mix
- Age and gender

Keep in mind that this information generalizes the entire population of the zip code. Be careful of depending too much on this information to make critical business decisions. Just because the majority of the zip code has a median income level of $50,000 does not mean that your customers necessarily fall within that income level.

For accurate Canadian census data, Statistics Canada (www.statcan.gc.ca) offers basic information for free; however, if you want detailed information for target group profiles, you will have to pay for it.

After you have completed the first table, you will have one perspective on your data. However, since you probably collected other information about your customers, you need to try to add that to your table. Continuing to add information to your table will show different ways to categorize the data. For instance, if you just do zip/postal code and age, you will get some information, but you may not get the entire picture. If you have the opportunity to gather more specifics about your customers, such as marital status or homeowner versus renter status, take the opportunity to include this information in your table and continue combining the information until you can clearly identify your customer groups. Table 2 includes gender to help you categorize your customers.

TABLE 2
CUSTOMER-TRACKING GRID INCLUDING GENDER

	18 – 30		31 – 50		51+		Total by Zip/Postal Code
	M	F	M	F	M	F	
Zip/Postal Code 1		I		I			2
Zip/Postal Code 2	II	~~IIII~~	III	IIII	I	II	17
Zip/Postal Code 3	III	~~IIII~~ II	III	~~IIII~~	II	III	23
Zip/Postal Code 4		III		II			5
Zip/Postal Code 5		I	I	I			3
	5	17	7	13	3	5	
Total by Age	**22**		**20**		**8**		**50**

You can now identify additional data from the new table:

- Customer gender: In Table 2 you can see that 35 of the 50 customers, or 70 percent, are women. Further, there are more female customers in each zip/postal code and age group. This also shows that a whopping 80 percent of the business' customers are women from the two closest zip/postal codes (i.e., Zip/Postal Codes 2 and 3).

Of course, there may be even more information to be gleaned from the data that has been collected. Try to keep manipulating and combining the various ways of looking at the data. Add in any other information you have until you have a clear picture of your customer information.

Once this is completed, the groups that contain the most customers will be the most significant. Identify two to six groups that describe at least 70 percent of your business. From Table 2, let's say you identified the following two groups as the most likely customers:

- Zip/Postal Code 2 (17 customers or 34 percent)
- Zip/Postal Code 3 (23 customers or 46 percent)

From this analysis you can tell that since 80 percent of your customers are in two zip/postal codes, you can focus your advertising and marketing campaigns in these areas.

Alternatively, you could have said that your customers are as follows:

- Women 18 to 30 (17 Customers or 34 percent)
- Women 31 to 50 (13 customers or 26 percent)
- Men 31 to 50 (7 customers or 14 percent)

If you are analyzing a marketing tool that targets women in your area, this analysis tells you that this marketing tool may be effective.

Depending on what you are looking to do, either of these groupings could be helpful. By having the information available in table form, you can complete whatever type of analysis you need. Even with this type of simple analysis you can already start to see where your customers come from. If you are trying to grow your business and increase your customers, you now have a better idea of whom to target.

Lifesaver: Markets, neighborhoods, and economies are never stagnant. As a result, customers, products, and competitors can change dramatically over the course of only a few months. Because of how fluid your market can be, customer demographic reviews should be conducted regularly — at least every six to eight months.

3.3 Find your most profitable customers

Knowing how many customers you have is valuable. It can allow you to focus your advertising on likely customers, but knowing just which customers are the most profitable is even better and makes new advertising even more profitable. Therefore, once you have these customer groups identified, you can now add some purchasing data to the information and see where the money really comes from. Go back to the tables you created and this time include:

- Items purchased (e.g., large purchase, small impulse buy, service contract)
- Margin on the purchase

This new result will now show an even more interesting picture. Using the information from Table 2, let's say you want to see which customers are most profitable. To do this, you will take the total margin on sales for all customers in that group and then divide it by the number of customers. This will show, on average, how much each customer in that group spends on purchases.

From this data, you are now able to gather additional information about your customers. You can see that women clearly spend more than men at this store. Further, you can see that the 18 to 30 age group consistently spends the most money at this business no matter the zip/postal code or gender of the customer. This new information can now allow you to further focus the direction of your business and your advertising.

After you collect the data you should be able to combine the customer types you have created with the purchases these types of customers make. The combination of the two types of data should tell you which group makes the —

- most frequent purchases,
- purchases that have the highest margin,
- least frequent purchases, and
- purchases that have the lowest margin.

Combining this data can give you some interesting information. For instance, you know from the customer information that women make up the majority of your customers. What you now can see is that in general, they are also the most profitable group. Similarly, if the men that were only 30 percent of your customer base were making significantly larger margin purchases than the women, you would need to analyze the impact this information could have on your business.

Once you know who purchases the most from your business and which customers have the highest margins, you have a good idea which customers make you the most money! Unfortunately, the customer group that has the highest margin may not always be the customer group that makes the most purchases. When you start looking at your current customer list, you may be surprised that they are not the group you were expecting. This may or may not be a problem.

If the groups make sense, but you were simply not expecting the information, that is fine. In the example of the children's clothing store, if you find that 20 percent of your customers

TABLE 3
CALCULATING HOW MUCH EACH CUSTOMER SPENDS

	18 – 30		31 – 50		51+		Total for Zip/Postal Codes
	M	F	M	F	M	F	
Zip Code 1		$15		$25			$40
Zip Code 2	$25	$35	$20	$25	$15	$22	$142
Zip Code 3	$24	$42	$19	$22	$10	$16	$133
Zip Code 4		$25		$15			$40
Zip Code 5		$23	$9	$19			$51
Total	$49	$140	$48	$106	$25	$38	$406

are grandparents looking for gifts for their grandchildren, that may be a surprise, but it also makes sense for a children's clothing store.

If you discover that 65 percent of your margin comes from customers who are outside your immediate area (e.g., county, zip/postal code, or town) this may be a concern. After all, why don't more locals shop at your business? Does your product price point match your local income levels? This is an important consideration because it may be more lucrative to try to sell to customers in your immediate area than it is to try to convince people to drive long distances to obtain your product or service. This will be an important decision for your business to make. Either you have to choose to focus your business on your current customer base, or you will need to redesign your advertising and marketing to expand your local customer base.

Lifesaver: Tracking customer information is most effective when it is done continuously. Having data over the course of months and even years can allow more detailed reporting. It may be possible to identify seasonal changes or subtle trends. The sooner these customer dynamics are identified, the sooner a business can start to respond.

4. How Effective Is Your Advertising?

Many businesses rely on a variety of marketing and advertising to increase sales and bring in new business. Unfortunately, not all business owners are aware of how well their advertising really works. Many businesses purchase advertising and then fail to track its effectiveness.

For example, when the economy is growing and customers are more likely to purchase products, some business owners see this increase in sales as being directly from their advertising. However, this may not be the case. In a growing economy, advertising can often be considered more effective than it really is. When the economy slows, it is likely that the business owners may be perplexed as to why their advertising has "stopped working." As a result, they continue to run the same tired ads to the same incorrect audience and spend thousands of unnecessary dollars. Some types of advertising you may be paying for include:

- Phone book listings
- Newspaper advertising
- Newspaper classified ads
- Small business journals
- Advertising on the back of supermarket receipts
- Radio spots

Each of these types of advertising can be valuable to the right business. In this case, the advertising will quickly bring in new customers and easily pay for itself.

One business owner we know just started a steam cleaning business. Although he only used a Yellow Pages ad to announce his business, he was able to grow quickly in the first year he was open. Yet there are other cases in which the cost of the advertising is disproportionate to the sales it generates. This can be due to many different reasons, but is very commonly from advertising to the wrong audience with the wrong message.

4.1 Check your advertising demographics

Since you know what type of customers your business attracts, it is now possible to determine if you are using the right advertising for your company. For each type of advertising that your business utilizes, find out exactly what type of customer demographic is being targeted. To do this, call your vendors and ask them to provide you with a detailed list of their target demographics. They should be able to provide information about how many people see your ad each time it is displayed, the general characteristics that describe these viewers (e.g., age, location, income level), and what type of responses other businesses have from their advertising. Press the vendors to be as specific as possible.

Once you have this information, determine if each method of advertising is focused at targeting the customer group that is most profitable for your business. Mailers, for instance, tend to target local homeowners more than the average teenager, while online advertising on networking sites will reach more young people than baby boomers. Now that you know your most profitable group, you can understand why advertising is either working or not working. For instance, one company we know was spending money placing classified ads in the local Spanish language newspaper. Since the business was not located in a Spanish-speaking neighborhood and only had one employee that spoke Spanish, they received very little traffic from this source. Once they checked the number of customers, the margin on those customers, and the cost of the advertising, it made sense to drop this advertising.

Next, check the ads themselves. Do they appeal to your current profitable customer groups? If the advertising source isn't working very well (bringing in some customers, but not many), you may want to try some slight modifications. Small changes could make an advertising source change from borderline to profitable if used correctly.

Try to make sure that your ad is customized to your market. Many advertising companies will work hard to retain their clients. Some offer free marketing consulting and will even redesign your ad for free if you let them know it is not receiving the results you expected.

4.2 Tracking advertising effectiveness

When you ask small-business owners which type of advertising is the most profitable, many of them don't know. Business owners sometimes spend thousands of dollars each month on ads that don't work or spend money on ads that are more expensive than they need to be. In some cases, even businesses with sales and marketing teams may not be able to answer this question. The reason is that many people believe that any advertising is good for the business even if the advertising results in no sales! Since the main purpose of advertising and marketing is to grow your business, analyzing this customer data will let you know much more clearly what type of advertising is bringing in customers and from where.

To identify the effectiveness of your advertising, you need to understand which advertising brought which customers to your business. For large businesses with national marketing campaigns, the individual business at each location doesn't usually care about this type of information. Since the brand spends millions each year on advertising, the assumption is that the main office is also reviewing the effectiveness of the advertising. However, this isn't the case for small businesses. If your business isn't a franchise and doesn't rely on national campaigns, it's up to you to know how well your advertising really works.

Therefore, the one question you should ask whenever customers purchase anything from your business is, "How did you find out about us?". You can then track their answers against advertising. There are also two options that businesses should always include in their tracking:

- Repeat customer — for customers that have returned to your business and aren't responding to an ad.

- Customer referral — for those customers that were referred by other customers (don't include business partner referrals in this group, list these as a separate category).

A simple way to see this is to use a grid, such as in Table 4.

After a few days or weeks, you should begin to have enough data to start understanding where your customers are coming from. With only 40 sales shown in Table 4, it is already possible to see where the customers for this business are coming from. It's obvious that repeat customers and customer referrals are bringing in the most purchasers, while magazine advertising has brought in no customers during this same period. In this case, the local newspaper is much more effective than the phone book and the phone book is much more effective than magazine ads. With that information in hand, you can begin to rank the effectiveness of your advertising. If you assume that you spent the same amount on all three advertising areas, you can now tell which one is most effective.

TABLE 4
TRACKING YOUR ADVERTISEMENTS' EFFECTIVENESS

Advertisement	Number of Customers
Repeat customer	HHI HHI IIII
Customer referral	HHI HHI II
Local newspaper	HHI II
Phone book	II
Supermarket receipt	HHI
Magazine advertising	

In general, you want to make sure that you track this information long enough to get a clear picture of your customer base. For instance, if magazines are delivered at the beginning of the month and you are doing this study in the last few days of the month, your impression of the effectiveness of your magazine advertising may be misleading. Therefore, take a few weeks — preferably a month or more — before you draw any serious conclusions from your statistics.

However, this is just the beginning of the type of analysis you can do. Very rarely does all advertising cost the exact same amount, and oftentimes, different advertising brings in different types of customers. For instance, are the customers who find you in the phone book more likely to make larger or smaller margin sales than the customers who find you in the newspaper?

> # WARNING:
> Before committing to a long-term advertising contract make sure to arrange a short trial period. Even if a trial period is offered at a higher rate, testing advertising before you commit to a long contract will provide time to track the results of the new ads. If the advertising is not effective, you can then drop the ad without being committed to a long-term contract.

4.3 Find the *real* cost of all your advertising

Now that you know how many customers are brought in by each method of advertising, you have one piece of information — but you can also expand your table to get even more information. By including the types of products the customers purchased, you will now be able to see the average margin for each type of advertising. From there you can discover the cost of bringing a customer in to your business. This information allows you to compare advertising methods and discover which type of advertising brings in the most profitable customers. There are two calculations you need to find for each of your advertising sources:

- Cost per customer: This calculation tracks how much it costs to bring in a customer using a given advertising method. Finding this value is simple once you know where all your customer sales come from. Just get the monthly cost of the advertising type and divide it by the number of customers. For example, if you pay $400 for a classified ad in your local newspaper and 22 paying customers tell you they came in because of that ad, you have spent $18 per person to get each of those customers.

- Margin per customer: Next, determine how much margin (or profit) you make on each customer broken down by source. Once you have identified that there were 22 paying customers from the advertising source all you have to do is determine the margin on each of their sales. To find the margin on each sale, just take the gross sale prices (i.e., the total amount the customers paid excluding any sales tax) and subtract the costs of the products or services they purchased. For instance, if the 22 paying customers' purchases totaled $1,500 in gross sales and the costs of those products were $796, the total margin is $704 and your margin per customer is $32. The formula would be:

  - $1,500 (gross sales) − $796 (product cost) = $704 (total margin)

- $704 (total margin) ÷ 22 (customer total) = $32 (margin per customer)

Once you have these two numbers, it is easy to determine if each of your advertising types is worthwhile. A typical table may look something like Table 5 once it is completed for the month.

In this example spending $400 on your local newspaper ad has brought in $704 in margin for a net profit of $304. Obviously, this advertising is effective and worth keeping. When you do this exercise, you will probably find some sources are fairly obvious revenue generators. From Table 5, it is clear that the local newspaper is the most effective. Of course, other types of advertising are not as clear-cut. For instance, what about the phone book ad that costs $200 and only brings in $208? In this case the business may want to keep the advertising since it can generate a significant number of return customers and referrals.

As a rule, whenever a high percentage of customers return or your business has a high number of referrals, any advertising source that breaks even month-to-month will make your business money over the long run. Our business had one magazine ad like this. It was a small magazine that was a staple for many local businesses. The advertising cost to place an ad in this periodical was significant and at most, we would receive only one or two calls from the ad each month. However, since the few calls we did get were from businesses that wanted to make large purchases, the advertising was considered a worthwhile investment, as just one response generally paid for the ad for that month. Each additional purchase made by the business in the coming months was all profit.

What if your advertising investment brings in less money than it costs? Even with results that are lower than breakeven, it is still possible that the advertising is worthwhile. For instance, if you recently purchased the advertising, you may find that it will take a while to reach the audience. In this case, you may need to wait a few weeks or even months before you can tell if the advertising is bringing in customers or not. However, before you make any decision to drop advertising, you must complete detailed research to determine if you are making up this money in any other way (e.g., customer referrals, return visits). However, odds are good that this type of advertising is not as effective as it should be and may be a candidate for cancellation.

TABLE 5
COST AND MARGIN OF ADVERTISING PER CUSTOMER

Advertisement	Monthly Cost	Number of Customers	Cost per Customer	Total Margin	Margin per Customer
Repeat customer	$0	45	$0	$1,575	$35
Customer referral	$0	36	$0	$1,404	$39
Local newspaper	$400	22	$18	$704	$32
Phone book	$200	13	$15	$208	$16
Supermarket receipt	$300	5	$60	$110	$22
Magazine ad	$375	0	n/a	n/a	n/a

Moneymaker: Free online advertising is a great way to bring new customers into your store. Some local newspapers offer free advertising either in their paper or online. Other sites are dedicated to free advertising. Our favorite, Craigslist.org, is available throughout the US and Canada and is completely free.

4.4 Cancel your ineffective advertising

Once you understand who your customers are, what they are buying, which ones are the most profitable, and what your advertising effectiveness is, odds are good that you will also be able to tell what advertising is the least effective. Typically, ineffective advertising will not pull in many customers or will simply cost more than the customers it draws can purchase. If changing your ads hasn't worked, it may be time to admit that some types of advertising just don't work for your business.

When we did the same exercise at Arizona Computer Outlets, we found that we received no referrals from supermarket receipts. We spent about $3,500 on a program in which we placed coupons on the back of receipts at a large, local grocery store. We had spoken to other computer store owners who had good luck with this avenue and thought it was worth a try. It wasn't. In the year that we tried the program, we had three people come in and not one of those three people spent more than $100. After the contract was up, we chose to cancel this type of advertising.

For classified ads, we found that we were getting customers, but not as many as we expected for the money we were spending. It turned out the ad was generating quite a few calls but not many sales. Because of the volume of calls, we thought it was effective, but when we compared the calls to the actual number of people coming in, we realized we were wasting money. Beyond that, the calls added additional unnecessary work for our team. As a result we reduced the ad significantly. Cutting supermarket receipts and modifying our classified ads saved us thousands of dollars each month and had little if any impact on the number of new customers our business had each month. Without customer tracking, we would not have known we needed to make changes.

WARNING:

Many business owners cancel advertising when times are tough. Unfortunately, this is often when they need it most. Advertising can help expand your business quickly and effectively, especially during a down market. Before you remove advertising money from your budget you may want to try rewriting the ad or trying a different type of ad.

4.5 Increase your best advertising

Now that you know where your best customers are coming from it may be possible to increase your advertising and get even more customers. Just be careful how you approach this. While an ad in the Yellow Pages may bring in some customers, adding a second ad doesn't mean you'll double the response.

Another way to increase your advertising is to find new opportunities that are as similar as possible to your most effective advertising. For instance, if you found that a local magazine ad was effective for your business, start researching what other magazine advertising is available in your area. Here are some questions you should ask before committing to work with an advertiser:

- What demographics do you serve? Get as many specifics as possible. Distribution, viewer age, addresses, and household income should all be included in the answer.

- Do you have any other advertising for a company that is similar to, or the same as, my business? Ideally you don't want to compete in overly saturated advertising. Your goal is to get customers, so why advertise in the same space as a few dozen businesses just like yours?

- What response rate have businesses like mine found? Many periodicals and advertising companies have branches in various locations. As a result, it may be possible to see how a company in a similar type of work did using their advertising. Also, ask to see what types of ads the similar company ran.

- What assistance do you provide making my ad? Ask for assistance up front to get new ideas and ensure that your ad fits the customer interest of the new advertising source.

- What is the minimum ad term I can purchase? Taking the shortest term possible will give you time to analyze the results of the advertising. Although it may be more expensive than signing up for longer terms, the value of being able to cancel a source that brings in no customers will be worthwhile.

4.6 Track brand loyalty

Now that you know what advertising brings in customers, you also want to check that your customers are coming back. Getting customers to your store or interested in your business is a difficult and costly exercise and once you have them there, you want to ensure they continue to come back.

Each business has a different way that they can create customer loyalty. Even stores that specialize in large, unusual purchases (e.g., projector televisions or pools) can expand their product line to bring back their customers. For instance, a local flooring store specializes in new floor treatments. Typically, these are large purchases that don't need to be done more than once. However, they also sell specialized cleaning products that are made especially to "protect your investment in your home." Even though the customer won't buy the same flooring product for the same location in the near future, they may continue to come back for the cleaning product, which is another source of income for the business.

Moneymaker: Make it easy for customers to make repeat purchases. In just about any business, there are ways to do this. For example, some salons ask customers if they want to "schedule their next appointment" as the customer pays the bill. At our store, we track the customer's printers so that we can help them find their ink the next time they come in. Whatever your business, you should find at least one way to make it easier for your customers to complete repeat purchases.

4.7 Referrals = free advertising

Most people enjoy helping a friend who is having a problem by referring the person to a credible business. This type of advertising is invaluable as the customers who were referred are more likely to buy because they already know and somewhat trust your business. However, if the number of customer referrals your business has is low, you can be sure that customers are not happy with your service or products and are not recommending your business to their friends. If this is the case, this valuable information will allow you to focus your time and effort on improving the customer experience.

Some very successful small businesses have never paid for an ad. One chiropractor we know opened his business around 2000. He found a storefront in a strip mall, signed a five-year lease, put up a simple sign that read "Chiropractor" and opened his door. Within a few years, he had a full client list, was working three and a half days a week, and supporting his wife and children without ever spending a nickel on advertising.

How did this chiropractor build his business? Referrals. Each of his customers is very satisfied with his work. If you walk into his office and talk to any of the patients, all will give him rave reviews. Further, each person has his own story of how he or she "found" him. Usually, a friend whose life had been changed through chiropractic work recommended him and now he or she also uses him.

What makes this chiropractor so special? Any of his customers will be happy to tell you. He doesn't hurry or stick by a set amount of time. He works with each person to make sure he or she is satisfied, tracks the person's progress, and sometimes even turns customers away if they don't have a chiropractic problem. By delivering quality service he has managed to build a thriving business without any advertising at all!

9
KEEP YOUR CUSTOMERS AND CLIENTS HAPPY

Today, more than ever, increasing revenue requires building a strong sense of customer service. When money is tight, customers are reluctant to spend. Therefore, whatever your business model, the customer or client must be happy with the product delivery and the value they receive. Even when customers are not dealing directly with you or your employees, as in the case of online businesses, the customer is still getting an impression of your business and of your ability to deliver service. In a highly competitive market, where the same products are sold by hundreds if not by thousands of different vendors, customer service can make the difference between having a single customer who orders a product once and doesn't return, and incredibly loyal customers who will actively work to help build your business through referrals and repeat orders.

Never forget your fundamental responsibility as a business owner — you must quickly and efficiently deliver your goods and services to your customer. When services are not capably delivered or when the customer is not satisfied, it does not matter how successfully the business is run — to the customer, the transaction was a failure. Regrettably, whenever a business has unhappy customers, the effect is generally seen at the bottom line — revenues can plummet. This also means that one of the simplest ways to increase your revenue, without spending a dime, is to improve customer service.

There is no reason why every employee at your business should not always be focused on providing five-star customer service. Focusing on customer satisfaction consistently generates more repeat customer sales and more referrals. It enhances the business's reputation in the market and there are some unexpected benefits as well.

Customers who have a strong relationship with the business are less likely to sue the business or file a formal complaint. One of the industries in which this has been studied the most is the medical field. As far back as 1997, studies can be found that link a doctor's communication skills with his or her likelihood to be sued for malpractice. These studies consistently show that the most likely reason a physician is sued is not due to medical negligence, a lapse in care, or even a poor outcome, but it was actually traced back to how the doctor spoke with the patient.[1]

Similarly, in your business, there will be customers that do not get their products on time, have to deal with accidental human errors, or experience problems with the product or service. This does not mean that you have to have an unhappy customer. Some business owners can manage the relationships so well that even when a problem occurs the customer is still happy to allow the business to resolve the issue. When you have great customer service and a strong relationship with individual customers, they will be grateful at how the situation was resolved.

1. How Did You Treat Your First Customer?

The first step in handling a problem to the customer's satisfaction is to build a relationship with the customer the moment he or she walks in your door. Think back to your first customers. You were probably excited to make the sale. You wanted to give them a great impression of your store and wanted to ensure that they would become loyal customers for years to come. You greeted them with a smile, helped them find whatever they needed, and then finalized the transaction as courteously as you could. Each of these customers was probably very pleased with your business and maybe even became the loyal customers you hoped for.

After a business has been running for a while, that type of stellar customer service can slip away. The excitement of the first customer has been replaced by concern over getting more customers. The difficulties associated with ordering new products, paying bills, managing employees, and handling inventory has become much more difficult than it first appeared. New employees may have joined that don't yet put the same priority on customer service. However, to the customer that walks into your business for the first time, he or she is a "new customer" and the impression the person gets of your business will directly depend on the experience he or she has with your company that day.

To a new customer, there is no history. The person doesn't care about the difficulties a business encounters day-to-day. The customer doesn't wonder if the employee is new or old. He or she doesn't make allowances if the employee is just having a "bad day." To the customer, this is a one-time opportunity to discover if he or she likes your business or not. This decision will be made within the first few minutes of the person entering your business. Each customer should always be treated as though he or she was the first customer!

If you are busy, stop what you are doing! If you are unhappy, put those thoughts out of your head and smile. For that moment, with the customer, you or your employees are representing your business. The type of experience the customer has *at that moment* will decide if he or she will purchase something and come back again and again, or leave without buying anything and never return. Take the time to make sure that each customer has the "first customer" experience.

---

[1] The University of Chicago Medical Center, "Communication Skills Diminish Malpractice Risk," http://www.uchospitals.edu/news/1997/19970209-malpractice.html (February 19, 1997).

Lifesaver: When a customer walks into your store, pay attention to how he or she is greeted. The welcome the customer receives will create the customer's first impression of your business. A warm, friendly greeting can help build a strong relationship. Each customer should be greeted by a smiling employee whether in person or on the phone.

2. Always Deliver on Your Promises

When customers don't get what they want, it often seems as though they take it out on anyone who is nearby. That could be your employees, or you. Usually, it is whoever is giving them the bad news. Unfortunately, not everyone is good at conveying difficult situations to customers. One of the worst ways to prevent a problem is to try to tell the customers what went wrong. The customers don't care if your supplier failed to deliver. They don't care if the part was out of stock. They don't care if the item was lost in the mail. They don't care if an employee has a sick child at home. While they may make the appropriate sounds of concern, in truth, they shouldn't be inconvenienced by any of these issues. A customer doesn't want to work with a company they can feel sorry for; they want to work with a company that they can trust to deliver.

If your business cannot deliver on its promises, no matter the reason, in the customer's mind, you have failed to deliver. However, many employees and some business owners don't understand this simple lesson. Every problem a customer runs into is an opportunity for your business to stand out and increase its profitability. Take advantage of each customer complaint, problem, late payment, and difficult situation to increase your business, and become more competitive.

3. Become the Solution Provider of Choice

Customers always have problems. Even though in some cases these customers walked into your business with these issues, they are expecting that your business can provide a solution for them. This can be a difficult situation for a business. The only thing the customers really want is a solution, not a larger problem. Therefore, the only good way to present a bad issue to customers is to provide them with options to handle the problem.

For instance, with a computer store, we often run into situations in which a computer's hard drive fails during testing. Since the customer brought the computer to us because he or she was having issues, it is not unreasonable to assume that the hard drives may be the cause of their problems. Yet, this does not mean that the customer wants to learn that they have just lost all of their spreadsheets, family photos, and valuable documents. What they want is a solution to their problem. Therefore, instead of calling and telling them, "Sorry, your hard drive just failed and you lost everything," we call and offer them a service that can solve their problem. "Your hard drive has failed. We know how frustrating this can be and we see it all the time. Would you like us to try to do a data recovery and transfer your files to a new system?"

The difference in these two statements is significant. In the first statement, we have simply told the customers the problem they are facing and left them alone to handle it. They have no opportunity to resolve the issue. In the second, we offered them a solution to a problem they already suspected they would have. If you were a customer, which call would you prefer?

Therefore, before you present any problem to your customer, always have a solution prepared. If a product is late, and the customer needed it on a particular date, try to think of temporary alternatives that can meet the customer's needs. If a repair turns out to be more difficult than expected, do whatever you can to keep the costs within the customer's budget. By presenting a creative solution to a problem instead of just a problem, you will build trust with your customers and be able to become the "solution provider" of choice.

3.1 When customers want more

Very often, you will have customers that want more than you offer. You may have sold certain products or services, but the customer expects or wants additional items along with this original purchase. Take this as an opportunity for your business to grow. Each time a customer asks for something your business does not sell or a service you do not offer, the person is providing you with *free* product and service research for your target market.

You also are immediately provided with a test environment for the new product or service. If the customer is interested in making a purchase, you can test a pricing structure and implementation almost immediately. Plus, even if the new item is not successful, your business will have learned more about a new product, which you will likely be asked about in the future. The next time, you will either have a way of pricing and providing the service or a reasonable answer as to why you don't recommend it to your customers. Either way your business wins!

3.2 When customers complain

No matter how much you focus on service, no matter how much you build quality into your business model, every business has at least a few disgruntled customers. It has been said that an unhappy customer is much more likely to relate his or her experiences than a happy customer. Unfortunately, many business owners have found this to be true. Making up with customers who have had a bad experience can be a simple and an easy way to expand your sales.

Customers aren't asking for anything crazy. Most just want a good experience with reliable service and products that provide value. When they don't get what they want, most just walk away and never come back. Customers that complain are a rare opportunity. Think about it, when customers complain they are telling you *exactly* what their problem is. It's likely other customers have had the same issue but weren't comfortable telling you, so this is a golden opportunity to make your store better.

If you have a customer who has had a bad experience, take the time to understand his or her issue and explore solutions. Odds are the information the person provides will be invaluable and by resolving the customer's issues you may just gain a new loyal customer.

These individuals are so vested in the purchase that they are willing to take the time to tell you what went wrong. Although this may seem like a problem, these individuals are often great sources of information and, if handled properly, can even become loyal customers. The following are some rules that you must always follow when dealing with an unhappy customer:

- Do not take the customer's complaints personally. Most customers are upset, but not with you personally.

- Never let a customer's frustration make you angry or annoyed. If you yell at a customer or show hostility, you will never win the customer back and may lose other customers who witness the disagreement. Just stay calm. The customers will take their cues from you.

- Ask the customer what he or she feels would resolve the situation. You may not always be able to get the person what he or she wants, but you may be able to compromise. Suggest a resolution of your own if you can't meet the person's request.

- Try not to refund money. It is almost always better to resolve the customer issue with a new product or replacement service than it is to give the person back his or her money and have the person leave without anything. A person cannot be a satisfied customer if he or she hasn't made a purchase.

- Never let a customer leave angry, if you can avoid it. Not all customer issues can be resolved, but no customer should leave angry.

- Do not allow a customer to physically threaten you or your staff. While this doesn't occur often, you do not want to be involved in a physical confrontation. If you are unsure how to handle the situation, have someone call the police before the situation escalates.

One of the most incredible experiences we have had with Arizona Computer Outlets was with one customer, who we will call David. He came in unhappy with the previous owners and frustrated with the computer he had purchased. From this customer we were able to learn more about the past owners and their policies and practices. David was candid and clear and once he noticed that someone was listening to him, calm. We ended up resolving the situation by replacing the defective components. Although this was a costly decision (the business had to pay for the replacement parts) it was a good investment. David turned out to be a reseller who has continued to order up to five computers each month.

Working with the unhappy customers to resolve issues and difficulties they have can go a long way to improving your bottom line and your standing with customers. By always trying to work things out with disgruntled customers, our store has built a strong customer base and some of our most loyal customers are now customers that have had their complaints resolved.

Moneymaker: Put your customers to work for you! If you invest time in building a strong customer relationship, you can often use your customers to help build your business. If they like your work and want to "thank" you, ask them to take some business cards and give them out to a few friends. Customer referrals are invaluable and can quickly grow a business.

3.3 When customers pay late

There may be money to be found in your customer accounts. Take a look at the actual payments made on your sales in the last month. If you are running a retail store, it is likely that most of your sales are paid at the time of purchase. This means that you have very few customer bills that are awaiting payment or in accounts receivable. However, if you are running a service organization, or dealing with other small businesses, it is possible that you may have a few bills still unpaid.

There can be a number of reasons why there are unpaid bills. In tough markets especially, small businesses may be struggling and may not pay on time. However, another possibility may be that the customer is unhappy with the service or product provided and may resent the bill — as the saying goes, happy clients generally pay on time. Whatever the reason for the delayed payment, it can cause problems for your business. These chronic payment problems can wreak havoc with your cash flow and make it difficult for you to know when you can pay your own bills.

If you find that your business has an accounts receivable list, make a plan to start to focus on those accounts. There are many ways to quickly collect on these debts that will improve the customer relationship instead of stressing it further. Some businesses send out monthly invoices reminding customers of their debt. While this regular bill is very useful for a large company, small companies may struggle with the additional time and expense. The best way to approach a late payment problem is to actually speak with the business owner or customer to determine why the payment is late. This type of personalized service will allow the customers to communicate any problems they are having. The following are some options you can offer late paying customers:

- Facilitate automatic payments: If your customer has a monthly or other regular bill, you can offer automatic payments, even if your system is not equipped to handle this. Just obtain authorization (in writing) and run a customer's credit card manually each month. Although it may be manual, your business is probably more likely to complete this monthly payment than your chronically late customer.

- Provide a check pickup service: Just call ahead, let the client know you will be in the area and that you will be able to pick up a check. Many small businesses won't mind this courtesy and will be willing to pay on time. Make this a social call as well, checking on the customer's recent purchases and discussing any future needs. Although this additional work can be time consuming, having the cash in your bank account can make it worth the

effort. Further, if the customer is having a problem with the payment, it will allow you to find out about this situation before any additional debts are incurred.

- Offer to take partial payments: For some businesses, cash flow can vary. Sometimes a business will not pay a bill simply because they cannot pay it all at once. Offering to take a partial payment will reduce the debt, increase your cash flow, and show your customers that you are willing to work with them through difficult circumstances.

Even if you have resolved the immediate issue with the customer, make sure to note the customer's past late payments. If a customer is not paying you regularly, it is possible that this is the beginning of a bigger problem. Before you accept large orders from a customer with this type of history, you may want to ensure that the bill will be paid by requiring a significant portion up front.

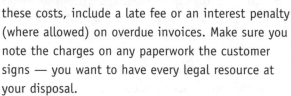

Moneymaker: When your customers fail to pay bills on time, your business may incur more costs than you realize. Additional postage, paper, envelopes, and time are all required each time an additional invoice is sent out. To offset these costs, include a late fee or an interest penalty (where allowed) on overdue invoices. Make sure you note the charges on any paperwork the customer signs — you want to have every legal resource at your disposal.

3.4 When customers stop paying

In a tough economy, the sign that bills aren't being paid on time may indicate that your customer is in a more difficult financial position than you realize. What you may find is that your customers are still ordering products and services even if they are no longer paying for their products. As a business owner, you may at first be excited that you have continued to make sales; you may even appear to be very profitable. However, if the customers are not paying their bills, it may be because they are in a difficult financial position and will go under before they can ever pay the bills. While this doesn't always happen it should always be considered a possibility.

Both small businesses and large Fortune 100 companies fall into the trap of selling to businesses just before they declare bankruptcy. Of course, there is no surefire way to tell the difference between a company that will be bankrupt soon and one that is just in a temporary difficult position.

One way to keep your customer's business and still hedge your risk is to make new sales under new terms. Instead of allowing the business to continue to purchase on credit, implement a credit maximum for your clients. Then sell them any new products only if they agree to pay new purchases by Cash On Delivery (COD). If you want, you can also ask the customers to pay COD on the new bill plus 10 percent of their outstanding bill. This will show your commitment to your customers, continue to bring in new sales, and not jeopardize your cash flow.

 **Lifesaver:** Under-promise and overdeliver. This old adage is valuable for any business. The easiest way to do this is to ensure each deal has enough wiggle room in both time and profit. Cut any deal too close and you will be unable to absorb the unexpected, and may find yourself losing money instead of making it!

4. What Type of Customers Do You Want?

Now that we have established how all customers should be treated, it is time to focus on making sure your business sells to only the type of customers that your business wants.

What type of customers do you want? Take a moment to consider. Many small-business owners think this is a difficult question to answer; however, there is only one type of customer that any business wants. All businesses want *profitable* customers. That is the only type of customer that any business should have. Yet, time and time again, business owners feel that they must accept any customer in any circumstance. It is simply impossible to succeed in this way.

4.1 Sometimes you have to fire your customers

You need to know what you are spending on your customers and you need to be able to "fire" customers if necessary. Profitability is necessary for any small business to stay afloat and if your offerings are losing your business money, they are probably not the right offerings for your business. While some large businesses boast loss leaders (e.g., milk in grocery stores) this does not mean that losing money will always gain you money. Service companies are more likely to suffer from this problem than businesses that sell products, although any business can have this issue. In some cases, customers are simply too expensive to maintain. These individuals may take up your time or your employees' time continuously and unprofitably. Although this does not happen frequently, it does happen to almost every business, both large and small. To identify if there are any customers you may need to fire ask yourself the following questions:

- Do any of your customers purchase standard products or services and then demand customized implementations at standard rates?

- Do any of your customers regularly monopolize employee time with long conversations, constant questions, and inquiries?

- Do any of your customers request product information, proposals, and support, and then purchase comparable goods from another vendor?

- Do any of your customers poach your employees and then reduce purchases?

- Do any of your customers try to renegotiate bills at the last moment or after they have failed to pay on time?

- Are any of your customers constantly dissatisfied with work, products, or purchases? Do they often ask to have a bill reversed or reduced for "poor service" or other unexpected complaints?

If you have customers that behave in unethical ways like those mentioned in the list, it is possible they are simply taking advantage of your stellar support service. In many cases, these individuals cost your company so much time and additional overhead the company will barely break even on their sales. In some cases, the time you spend on these individuals or business may be losing your business money each month! Therefore, a business that wants to be successful has the option to manage these customers more carefully. To do this, you must take control of the relationship and ensure that your business spends less time and money on these problem customers. If that doesn't work, the customer simply needs to be fired.

When you find you need to fire a customer, remember to maintain a polite, positive attitude. Do not get into details or fights, simply explain that the relationship is no longer profitable for your business and that at the end of the sale or contract, you will either need to stop selling to this customer or increase the price of the products or services. Most people will understand that a company cannot stay in business if they do not price their products to cover their costs. While this may not be what a customer wants to hear, your business is to serve profitable customers, not all customers. Firing these unprofitable customers can have an incredible value to your business because it —

- frees up the resources who were wasting time with unprofitable customers for the profitable ones,

- allows the business to focus on activities that increase productivity instead of focusing on managing problems and issues, and

- improves employee morale by eliminating the customers that are never satisfied and are generally discontent.

Many businesses who fire customers immediately realize a significant boost in productivity and profitability. The result of these changes means the business will be able to increase its profitability and reduce its overhead without any new costs.

10
MOTIVATE YOUR EMPLOYEES

There are many different levels of motivation. Some employees are motivated by their wish to keep their jobs and will do the least amount they can. Their work is shoddy, their attitude poor, and their output low. Employees have an endless list of excuses why something you've told them to do couldn't be done, shouldn't be done, is too expensive, or is best done by someone else. One of my favorite responses is to ask them this simple question, "If you were paid a bonus of $50,000 to complete this assignment, do you think you could do it?" This puts things in perspective for them. If that much money were at stake, they would find a way to do it. I remind them that doing what I want is a job requirement and that amount is on the line, business-wise. It's interesting to see the creative solutions the employees generate. It's just a question of motivation. In this economy, doing just enough to keep your job won't work. You and all your employees need to be putting forth all available effort. There's no room for slackers.

As your business grows, you may find the need to hire additional staff. However, with the additional help comes additional challenges and opportunities. Having resources to assist with regular business functions should free you to focus on more important items, but some business owners find that their time is overly focused on employee management issues. This cannot be your focus. If you are serious about growing your business, your team must have the right people doing the right things.

1. The Problems Associated with Overstaffing and Understaffing

Before you can determine if you have the right employees doing the right jobs, you need to determine if you have the right number of people for the amount of work you have. Your capacity can be described as the amount of work your company can handle. In general, the more resources you have, the more capacity you have. However, a more important question is, what is your volume of work? If you can match your capacity with your volume, you will find that your business will function more smoothly than when you are overstaffed or understaffed. The following sections discuss some symptoms of bad staffing.

1.1 Personnel problems

When people have too much or too little work to complete, you may find that gossip, complaints, and employee issues abound. When people have too little to do, they often have more time to make up rumors and speculate about their concerns about the business. Sometimes, afraid of downsizing, they will deliberately use lies and sabotage to attempt to secure their own position.

Of course, having too much work for too small a staff can also cause issues. The employees may be putting in too many hours and may resent the extra workload. In these cases, some of the best in the group may take jobs elsewhere.

1.2 Productivity issues

Productivity can suffer if a team is overstaffed or understaffed. Overstaffed teams tend to work slower than necessary and accomplish little, since there is little to be accomplished. A group in this position may not be motivated to work hard as they may not feel that there is enough opportunity for them to advance and be recognized.

Similarly, a group that is understaffed will also have productivity issues, although the causes are different. When teams don't have enough people to complete the assigned work on time, they may feel like there is no point in putting in the effort when the work will be late anyway. As a result, they may simply give up on making dates and delivering to customers instead of actually accomplishing the tasks on time.

1.3 Errors

Companies without enough resources to complete the work may find that employees rush through a task in order to get to the next one. As a result, there is not enough attention given to the details of the job. Rushing through work may result in customer errors and complaints.

Companies with too many people can also have errors. If there are too many people in an organization, the responsibility may be distributed among too many different individuals. Since no one is responsible, everyone may feel like an error doesn't reflect on them or their team and therefore isn't a concern.

 **Lifesaver:** Start a log of common business errors. While some items may have obvious causes (e.g., human error, honest mistakes), some root causes are harder to find. By tracking issues in a separate log, patterns that would otherwise go unnoticed are easier to observe. It will then be possible to identify and resolve small mistakes before they become large issues.

2. Determine If Your Company Is Overstaffed Or Understaffed

In most cases, you already have an idea of whether you are overstaffed or understaffed. Before you make any decisions, research the situation to confirm your suspicions. Get involved with your team on a daily basis (or if your organization is very large, with the managers). Take a look at what is being accomplished and ask individuals for their feedback. While some employees will be very honest with you, others may be more reserved about identifying issues. Let people know that your only goal is the betterment of the team. Regardless of how you get your information, you need to know your team.

Next, take a look at your company's history. Has your volume changed dramatically over the last few years? Has your staffing? The easiest way to get a picture of how your company is staffed is to attempt to create a graph that shows your capacity (i.e., number of employees) to your volume (i.e., amount of work). At its most fundamental, you can use your gross receipts as an example of your volume. While this is a very general way of reviewing your past history — it doesn't account for pricing changes, market fluctuations, regulation issues, or inflation — if your business has not had any dramatic changes, this high-level review will give you an overall impression of how much work you have handled in the past with how many employees. The more specific you are, the more value you will gain from this review.

You can compare your staffing to any measure of your company's volume. Some examples include your number of customers or clients; the number, types of services, and products sold; or even your business revenue. At this point you only need to determine if your business is overstaffed or understaffed, you should not make any staffing decisions from this review. That will come later.

3. Do You Have the Right Team?

Once you know how large your team should be, take a moment to review the individuals on your team. How did you go about building your team? Have you hired them over the course of years, or did you hire people as you needed

them? If you have built your team over time, you may need to review what each individual does today. Assumptions that were appropriate only a few years ago may no longer be valid.

To ensure you have the right team in place, start by making a list of each of your team members. Take a look at each person with a critical eye toward ensuring that they are in the right role. Are they still the right person for the position? For instance, if you hired a part-time bookkeeper a few years ago, do you still have the volume of work to support the position? Has new technology come out that may make this position obsolete? Is there another underutilized employee in your organization that could be doing this work instead?

If you consider each role and each position, you may find that some changes need to be made. This does not always mean that you will have to reduce your staff. Sometimes just moving resources to more appropriate positions will have a dramatic effect. Even transferring small pieces of someone's position to another resource may have significant savings. For instance, look at your higher-paid employees and consider each of their tasks. Could any of their work be completed by more junior, lower-paid employees? If so, moving this work to other resources can save your company money as well as allow your higher-cost assets to focus on work that's really important.

Lifesaver: Internal competitions can be an easy, fun way to motivate staff. Creating small contests that take anywhere from a few days to a few weeks to complete can be an enjoyable way to have the team focus on performance. Adding a small reward, such as movie tickets or a gift certificate can make the event even more fun.

4. Firing Employees Can Improve Morale

One of the hardest decisions a business owner can make is to let an employee go. Oftentimes, the employee has been with the company for a while and is just not performing as well as he or she needs to perform. Many managers often believe it is their fault for not being able to motivate the individual. As a result, a manager may try numerous ways of adapting to the person to try to get him or her to improve.

When this is unsuccessful, the manager often keeps the employee rather than dealing with the conflict. The manager may justify the decision by telling himself or herself that although the person isn't doing his or her best, it's still less expensive to keep the person than to train a replacement. However, the cost to the business can be significant. If a company is paying for individuals who are not performing, money is being spent unnecessarily. Further, customer service is usually also impacted. Customers that deal with a poor performer usually have a poor impression of the company. This type of bad example can cause lost sales and dissatisfied customers.

Unfortunately, this type of poor performance doesn't just impact your bottom line and your customers. A poorly performing employee can be detrimental to other employees' performance as well. For example, one company we know had an employee well-known as the weakest individual in the company. Keeping the poor performer and not addressing the performance issues had a very negative impact on the team. Weak workers believed that keeping this employee showed that poor results and apathetic work were accepted. High performers were unmotivated to produce results that they felt would not be rewarded or valued. Slackers felt that they could fly under the radar and not risk their paycheck, whereas hardworkers felt taken advantage of and overworked.

Allowing this one person to publicly perform poorly impacted almost every member of the team. After a team review, the management finally decided to address the issue. The individual was given an opportunity to improve; however, he was eventually terminated. The results were dramatic. Although many employees felt badly that someone had been fired, almost everyone appreciated the message it sent. The team felt that performance was once again being monitored and that good work had a chance of being recognized. Further, since weak performers were now being managed, work was now more evenly distributed. The team started performing better and tension dropped dramatically.

As a manager, firing people when necessary can also improve the company performance. If the team and management are no longer focused on employee issues, time can be more appropriately spent growing the company. Having the team focus on positive ideas such as growth and improvement rather than negative problems often changes the entire mood of an organization and can make the workplace a more enjoyable place to be.

5. Finding and Hiring New Team Members

You may find that your company actually needs to hire new individuals to handle your current workload. There are many low-cost, easy ways to find new employees who are interested in working for your business. While large companies tend to use the more expensive websites, such as Monster.com and Jobing.com, it is possible to get qualified, capable people without spending hundreds of dollars on an online posting. The following list includes some areas to look for employees:

- Local high schools and colleges: Many educational facilities have guidance offices that will advertise your position for no fee. The candidates you receive are generally new to the job market, but enthusiastic about learning.

- "Help wanted" sign: Many companies can fill vacancies by just hanging a "help wanted" sign in the window. These signs typically cost only a few dollars and will bring in candidates that are local.

- Low-cost websites: There are still many websites that allow job postings for free or little money. Craigslist.org accepts "gigs" (i.e., short-term positions) for free and charges a small fee for job postings (depending on location).

- Local newspaper: Classified ads are another low-cost way to find employees. Always check to see if your classified posting also appears on the newspaper's website.

- Employee referrals: Always let your current employees know you are hiring. They may be able to refer qualified candidates that will work well in your organization.

Wherever you get your candidates, make sure that each one submits a résumé for your consideration. If the individual can't take a few minutes to create a résumé, chances are he or she isn't serious about the position.

Moneymaker: Always be polite and positive with each of your interviewees. Be positive about your company and its position in the industry. Even if the individual does not get the job, the person or his or her family may be potential or current customers.

5.1 Before the interview

Once you have all the résumés, you will need to filter the candidates. Scan through the résumés. If anything stands out as either a big problem or a big benefit, highlight it and make a note. Don't worry about spending too much time on this activity — the goal is to get a general opinion of the individuals who applied. For individuals that look like they have the skills you need, place their résumés in a "Yes" pile. If there's anything you don't like about a résumé, make a note why and place the résumé in the "No" pile. Your decision-making process doesn't have to be logical — only you will know the things that are important to you and you should never ignore your instinct. The last pile is for those résumés that fall somewhere in between. Add any résumés you aren't sure of into the "Maybe" pile.

Once you have the résumés separated out, take a look through the "Yes" pile again. If you don't have enough "Yes" résumés, you can always check out the "Maybe" pile until you have at least 10 to 20 decent candidates.

Lifesaver: Keep written documentation on why you eliminated each applicant. If you are ever sued for discrimination, you can use these documents as evidence that your decision was fairly made. Remember having "more qualified candidates" is a valid reason to eliminate an individual.

After you identify the top 10 to 20 individuals, plan to complete a brief phone screening session first, instead of immediately jumping into the interview. When you interview a person, you or your employees will typically invest at least an hour with the interviewee. Don't waste your time with people you can eliminate quickly. Call the potential employees and take about 10 to 15 minutes to speak with them about their résumé. One of the best questions to ask is, "Tell me what you are working on right now." This open-ended interview question is not intended to be a trick or a technical test. It simply allows the individual to give an answer so that you can gauge their communication skills.

You would think this question is a bit of a "gimme," but you wouldn't believe the answers people have given us. One woman simply stated, "Nothing." When pressed, she began a tirade that lasted 15 minutes. She griped about being underappreciated and underutilized, talked about how much she hated her job, whined about her boss, and within about two minutes, completely destroyed any chance she had of working for us! Another time a candidate started describing his day in minute and excruciating detail.

Over the years, many candidates have been eliminated for poor grammar or other communication issues that were clear in the first five minutes. Imagine if we had wasted an hour with them in a one-on-one interview! Remember, you are looking for someone to join your team. Listen to their answers with critical attention to their communication skills. Ask yourself the following questions:

- Can you understand the answer?

- Was the person clear and to the point?

- Did you feel comfortable with what he or she chose to discuss?

- Would you be proud to have this person represent your company?

At the end of the phone screening, you will probably have eliminated at least half of the individuals you screened. It is now time to pick the top five and invite them to visit your office.

5.2 Preparing the candidate for the interview

To save your company time, make sure the candidates are prepared for the interview. When you call to schedule the onsite interviews, take a few moments to make sure the candidates are aware of the following:

- Dress code: If your business has a dress code, make sure to communicate this to the candidates. You will want to make sure that they can present themselves appropriately. If they do not appear presentable at the interview, chances are they will not dress any better after a month or two of working with your business. Also, you can use this aspect to judge how savvy the job seekers are. You can choose to tell them nothing about your dress code and see how they look when they show up. If they are really motivated, they may go to your office before the interview and watch how people dress.

- Job salary: Find out what the candidate's last salary was or current salary is. If this salary is much higher or too much lower than what you are offering, odds are good this is not the right candidate for the position.

- Benefits: Be up-front if benefits are offered and determine if the person has received benefits of any sort in the past.

If the candidate is uncomfortable with any of these items, you may not want to continue with the interview process. Nothing is worse than hiring an employee who is dissatisfied with your company's package before he or she even starts! Although many unemployed people will take positions that pay less money than they believe they deserve, few will stay longer than it takes to find another, better job.

WARNING:

Before any employee participates in the interview process, make sure he or she is aware of all important guidelines regarding interview best practices. There are some questions that should never be asked during an interview. A great resource for discrimination guidelines is the US Equal Employment Opportunity Commission or the Canadian Human Rights Commission.

5.3 Interview tips

Once you find the candidates that you want to meet, make sure to take the time to conduct a thorough interview. Remember, you only have a short time to make a decision about how well the person will work with your organization. The following are some ways to ensure you always get the type of employees you need for your company:

- Plan a list of questions before the interview.

- Take at least an hour to interview the candidate, which allows enough time to let the conversation flow naturally.

- Have the candidate complete any technical tests or interviews to verify his or her skills prior to your meeting with him or her.

- Have at least two or three other company employees meet the individual — especially if this candidate will be working with those people a significant portion of the time.

- Let the candidate meet your team. If any of your team vetoes the person, don't hire him or her.

- If you need more time or want another opinion, don't hesitate to schedule another interview.

Remember to remain flexible during the interview process. You want to make sure that you gather all the necessary information to make a decision about the candidate. If the interview runs over, or changes course, accept the new direction, as long as you're getting valuable information. But don't allow the person to run the interview. You are establishing your place in the company the moment you speak to the person.

5.4 Never hire the "best" candidate

After you are done with your interviews, you should have an idea of whom you want to hire for the position. You should never settle for the person who is the best of the group if the person isn't the best for the position. If the best candidate isn't good enough, don't be afraid to start again. Repost the listing if necessary. Be more specific about what you are looking for, or possibly offer a higher salary if your candidates are not qualified enough. The cost of hiring the wrong employee can be a very expensive mistake and can easily cost more than adding a few thousand dollars to a position to get the right person. It's so tempting to just take the person who seems like he or she would be decent in the position rather than starting all over again. Take the time, you'll be happier in the long run.

6. Branding Your Team

Once you have a team, it is important to build unity within the group. A simple way of doing this while also building your brand is to have your team wear similar outfits. Even if you don't want to go as far as requiring a uniform, you can save money by requiring clothes that match. One local restaurant allows all the servers to wear any white shirt they want with a pair of black pants. The appearance is a very clean look that makes the staff look very uniform. At the same time this type of flexibility is beneficial because the employees can purchase their own clothes and choose their own styles.

However, if you want a more cohesive look, a low-cost way to do it is to get your employees company shirts. To choose a good shirt you should always look for the following:

- Professional style: While some businesses may like polo shirts, for others a simple T-shirt is more appropriate. Make sure the style of shirt you choose appears professional and is consistent with your line of business. A collared polo shirt is usually a safe option for most companies.

- Breathable fabric: Some materials are too warm for employees. Therefore, always look for shirts that will be on the cool side. Employees that are cold can add a company jacket or pullover, but employees that are too warm will have no options. Who wants uncomfortable, cranky employees?

- Clean color: Choosing a color is more than just matching your company logo. Make sure to think about what the employees will be doing while wearing the shirt. If they are in a position where the shirt is likely to get dirty, choose a dark color so that they always appear presentable.

- Durable logo: If you choose a company uniform, it is valuable to add a company logo to help build the brand. Depending on your brand, you can choose to either have a printed image on the center of the shirt or, if you are looking for a more professional, upscale appearance, a small logo embroidered on the shirt.

Just remember to get your team the appropriate number of shirts. If they don't have enough to get through their workweek, they may "reuse" the shirts without the proper cleaning in between.

7. Build a Championship Team

Everyone wants to be part of a successful, winning team. The positive energy and excitement makes it fun to get out of bed in the morning and go to work. The team needs to have a sense of unity. You and your employees are all working together to beat the competition and grow your customer base. Make sure everyone knows who your competitors are and how they are doing. Let the team know what your business goals are and make sure everyone knows what they can do to contribute.

Encourage your employees to work together as a team. Remind them that the business's success is more important than being right or wrong. This can take many forms depending on the organization. One way to implement teamwork is to start a ten-minute rule. If an employee is dealing with a problem for more than ten minutes, he or she is required to ask for help from another team member. This type of encouragement can build bridges between team members and teach employees to learn from each other.

If possible, you may want to also institute two holiday parties — one in the summer (e.g., a local barbecue), and the other around the holidays, at the end of the year. Some business owners throw these events at their home and serve at the party themselves. This is a nice, low-cost way to reward some of the hard work your team has put in over the year.

11
MANAGE YOUR PROBLEM EMPLOYEES

A company can succeed much more easily when everyone is working together and is helping to shoulder common tasks. While everyone in our business is important and we certainly value their contributions, that doesn't mean that they are free to go their own way, pursuing their own agendas. It's even more critical when the economy has slowed.

It is important to keep employees following the company's goals and objectives. If individual employees believe they don't have to adhere to company policies, these seemingly small slights can eventually become large, unmanageable problems. What begins with only one employee can eventually spread throughout the employee base. Therefore, any problems must be addressed or the conflict will simply continue to grow and get worse. Eventually, it could even risk the success of the business.

1. When Good Employees Turn Bad

When you first build your team, you believe that you have a strong, solid foundation to grow your business. Over time, almost every business owner will find that employees do not always remain loyal to the business or the business owner. This perceived betrayal may be harder on some owners than on others. It's largely a question of how involved you have been in supporting and assisting your employees. You may find you feel anywhere from surprised and disappointed to downright betrayed and hurt.

One of the most amazing employee stories we heard was from one owner who spent many years building his business. He built it from the ground up. What began as a small one-man shop eventually became a thriving operation. He was dedicated to both his business and his employees and always tried to help his people whenever possible.

One of his employees had been with him for years. No one in this employee's family had ever gone to college and the owner wanted to change that. He paid for the employee's child's entire education, attended the graduation, and was considered to be part of the family.

You can imagine his surprise when this long-time employee unionized his business! The owner felt betrayed and confused. He had gone out of his way to help this man and this man's family and this was how he was repaid? Fortunately, this story has a happy ending as the same employee that started the union also helped eliminate it.

While it is valuable to have a strong relationship with your employees, business owners also have to understand that an employee's first priority is usually his or her family and self-interest. Therefore, there will be times when you find that your loyal employees are suddenly asking for more or worse yet, demanding the impossible. In this case, you have to try to separate your friendship with your employees and avoid taking this conflict personally.

2. Confronting Conflict

Sooner or later you will realize that you have an employee that cares more about his or her own self-interest than he or she does about the business's survival. After all, it's your business and it's just not reasonable to expect your employee to have the same level of dedication and interest in it as you do. The only reason the person works for you is to get paid, and there's nothing wrong with that.

The problem emerges when employees believe they are worth more to the company than they really are. As a manager, you're constantly encouraging your employees, telling them they're doing a good job, praising their efforts, and keeping them motivated. However, this positive feedback can sometimes cause your employees to have an unrealistic perception of their value to the company. Perhaps they have friends who make more than they do and they are jealous. Maybe customers have told them they are the reason the company is succeeding. Maybe they just believe they have worked hard and deserve more.

No matter what the cause, it is possible to wind up with an employee who thinks that you are a greedy, money-grubbing thief and you are taking advantage of him or her. The following sections discuss why an employee may think this and how you can deal with it.

Moneymaker: Make sure that any past employee who receives unemployment payments actually deserves them. Your business pays money into unemployment insurance, not the employee. The more often your ex-employees receive unemployment, the higher your unemployment rates will be. If you have fired someone for cause, make sure to alert the unemployment division when a claim is made and attach any relevant, supporting documentation.

2.1 Employee complaint 1: I am irreplaceable!

There are often positions in a company that are not shared by multiple employees; this is especially true in a small business. As a result, many small-business employees eventually believe that they are irreplaceable. This is unfortunate in that it can sometimes make the employee difficult to manage. Business owners concerned about their businesses sometimes allow these individuals to have more control than they would like simply because they buy into the perception that one employee is truly critical to the business's success.

Think of your company and your employees. If someone comes to mind, you need to fix this immediately. No one should ever be in a position in which his or her departure would harm your company. If someone is so important that he or she can't leave, the position is not documented, managed, or tracked enough and the organization is at risk. Even if that employee would "never leave," circumstances are sometimes beyond anyone's control. If the employee becomes ill, or if his or her spouse gets an attractive job offer in another city, you may find yourself needing to replace the person in a hurry. You must not allow yourself to be in the position in which your business could lose money over one employee's departure.

Therefore, before you face this situation, you need to protect yourself. Take a critical look at each of your employees and think about what each person does. You need to consider how you would replace them. If you find that you don't know what an individual does, or that you would have no way to replace him or her, the first thing you need to do is document the position. Have the employees make a list about what they do each day and how they do it. If you have detailed documentation on a job, you will have some peace of mind if anything goes wrong.

Lifesaver: If you think that you are the employee that cannot be replaced, take the time to fully document what you do and how you do it. If you become ill, or cannot work, you will need to ensure that your business can continue to function. To test what could happen, take a week off. Any items escalated to you during this period are good examples of what tasks or processes need to be better documented.

2.2 Employee complaint 2: I am underpaid!

When you are in a competitive market, your employees will also know your position and may use this knowledge to gain more benefits. When a business is struggling, some people will want to take the opportunity to ask for more money, feeling that they have you over a barrel and you will be unable to say "no." Others believe that since your business has been successful, they deserve more money. There are also some people that will feel that it has been X amount of time, therefore they deserve a raise.

Whatever the reason, this situation can be very difficult. Some people will just request money and if you say no, they will accept it and keep working. Others will have outward or passive reactions. The difficulties these tense situations cause may lead you to believe that it is easier to give a nominal raise than to deal with yet another problem.

Before you make this decision, you need to critically consider the cost of keeping the employee against the cost of replacing the employee. Giving into demands like this can cause some long-term problems. Therefore, before you make the decision to give in and give the employee a raise, make sure that you don't fall for some of the following common traps:

- Don't increase your overhead unnecessarily. Increasing any employee's salary or benefits will increase your costs more than you may realize. When you increase a payment to an employee, you also increase your tax liability and unemployment payments. If you choose to provide a raise, make sure that it is necessary and that it is consistent with market rates.

- Don't set a bad precedent. When an employee believes that he or she can get more by complaining, it sets a precedent that may cause the person to continually gripe for more. While this may begin as a well-needed raise, the effect can cause complaints about everything from the benefits package to the coffee creamers!

- Don't assume that the problem is gone. Studies have found that employees that ask for more money and threaten to quit usually stay with the company only six more months before they leave anyway. The findings suggest that employees that are willing to quit basically want to quit and are just looking for an excuse. This means that while a raise may be a short-term bandage, you should be prepared to refill the position in a short time.

- Don't believe that a raise will stay a secret. Think about how the other employees would feel if they found out about the new rewards for just one individual. While employees are not supposed to reveal their salary information to others, it is a very rare company that has this type of secrecy. Therefore, if you are going to give a raise, be prepared for the rest of your staff to find out. Soon, you may have others begin asking for more as well, so consider whether you can you afford to increase salaries for everyone.

Of course, having an employee ask for money is not always a bad thing. For example, an employee with special skills asks for a 30 percent raise. Although the employee is skilled, it may not be reasonable to pay the person more, especially if the market for his or her skill has actually declined over the previous year. The employee may counterpoint that his or her ability has increased during the same period, but it may not have increased in value

to the business. In this situation, you could research re-staffing the position and find out whether the current, competitive salary to hire a new employee with the same technical skills is lower than what you are paying the current employee. If it is lower, you may explain this to the current employee and turn down the raise request.

Lifesaver: Sometimes it can be difficult to determine the fair market salary for a position. One simple way to check the market is to post the position with your estimated salary, on an inexpensive job posting board such as Craigslist.org. From the number of résumés you receive and the qualifications of the applicants, you will quickly be able to tell if the salary you posted is in line with the market or if you are paying too much or too little.

In the end, the employee may choose to leave. Your business may be more successful because of this personnel change. The new hire could save your company money because the person would be hired for less pay than the former employee and still have the same skills to do the job just as effectively.

When an employee asks for a raise, it is his or her responsibility to justify the raise. The questions you need to ask the employee are, "Why are you worth more to the company than you were before? How are you making the company more money than you were before?" Let's take as an example someone who bags groceries. That job is worth minimum wage. At any given time, you can hire someone to put groceries in a bag and no matter how long a person is in that position, the job is still worth minimum wage. If someone wants more money, the person needs to take on more responsibility and perform tasks that justify paying him or her more. As I have said on many occasions, "If you want to be paid more, you need to be worth more. Show me what you're going to do to make the company more money so I can pay you more."

2.3 Employee complaint 3: I know better!

As a business owner, it is sometimes necessary to change your business to adapt to the market and to meet competitive changes. You have access to the books which means that you can immediately tell when your income starts to slow. Regularly speaking with clients and customers will give you ideas for new products and services. However, you may find that your employees are not always as aware of these market changes as you are. As a result, when you try to implement suggestions, you may encounter some reluctance to adapt the changes you want to make. There can be many reasons for this. Employees often feel that since they are the individuals executing the ideas that they know better than you. Sometimes they are right, so it is always worth hearing them out; however, sometimes your big picture view may allow you to see opportunities and potential improvements that others may miss.

When we started to completely revamp our store, we hit a great deal of reluctance. Although we were implementing the best practices that we learned from many business owners, other individuals in our business were unhappy with the changes and were unenthusiastic about participating. While in some cases, the feelings may have been understandable, in others, the responses we received were simply overruled.

In the end, it is you, the owner, that fails if the business fails, and you have to deal with the consequences of the failure. Most employees will simply move on to positions at other companies. They won't lose their houses, their cars, or their lifestyles. Therefore, it is up to you to make the changes you think are necessary, even when the changes don't come easily.

When you receive a negative response, be prepared for a more difficult road to implementing your changes. If you are serious about improving your business, you will need to work through the employee complaints proactively. Odds are that if they do not want to complete the new tasks, you will find that these new jobs are pushed to the bottom of everyone's day. There will always be excuses why the unpleasant jobs aren't done. Therefore, when you are making changes, make sure that you don't do too many at once and that you stay on top of them until they are completed.

Taking the time to check on the execution of every task on a regular basis may seem silly, but it may be necessary to make everyone aware of how serious you are about the changes. After being met with resistance on cleaning the store, we found that verbal instructions were not working. Instead, we had to make a daily chore list for every cleaning task we expected completed. Items such as emptying the trash, vacuuming the floors, and dusting the counters were all painstakingly listed. We then assigned a person to complete each task and asked them to sign off when the tasks were done. At first, we found that the tasks were not being completed and had to "call out" each employee for not completing the work. However, after a few weeks, it eventually became routine. Although we no longer have to use such a detailed implementation plan, having it to begin with was a necessary part of making sure the cleaning was completed to our standards.

2.4 Employee complaint 4: I bring in the customers!

After employees have been with your business a few months or a few years, chances are they will start to develop relationships with your customers. They may know your big customers by name, remember their more common orders, and even know information about their families. Sometimes, employees believe that this relationship is the reason that some customers come into the store in the first place and without them the business would fail. Fortunately, this is rarely the case.

Most customers appreciate good customer service and some will even be disappointed when an employee leaves, but most customers will not change their shopping patterns just because one employee moves on. There are, of course, some businesses in which customers will follow an individual (e.g., doctors, hairstylists), but even in these situations, it is possible to retain customers when an employee transfers companies.

To ensure that the business will retain customers during any employee transition, make sure to follow these simple steps:

- Do not let your "leaving" employee have private conversations with your customers. Even when an employee is leaving of his or her own accord, it is possible that he or she may still take the opportunity to malign your business, either intentionally or unintentionally. There are many ways this may happen. An employee may innocently mention what competitor he or she will be working for; he or she may air your dirty laundry by saying why he or she is leaving; or he or she may make comments about how inexperienced his or her replacement is. Whatever the case, conversations like this can cause you to lose business and should be avoided. If this does occur, you may be better off providing two weeks paid leave rather than having your customers scared off by an unhappy employee.

- Do not allow employees access to your customer lists. One big risk is to allow employees to have the ability to print or copy your full customer list (e.g., names, addresses, and phone numbers). As soon as an employee has this information it is possible for him or her to use this as a contact list to pull your customers to a new business. Since it is never possible to know which employees may have aspirations of starting a competing venture, it is best to simply make sure that no employee has access to this very valuable information.

- Continue to provide wonderful customer service. When employees believe a customer is coming to your business for him or her, chances are it is because the customer appreciates the service that is provided. Therefore, the easiest way to make sure that customers are not lost during a transition is to ensure that high quality service is provided by all your employees at all times.

- Train new employees thoroughly before they deal with customers alone. Whenever a new employee is brought on board, make sure he or she is trained or at least paired with an experienced employee before working alone with customers. This will ensure that the customers continue to receive consistent service that meets your company's standards and will reduce customer frustration.

3. Take Proactive Steps to Prevent Sabotage

Just because your employees haven't said anything to you about their pay or their function doesn't mean that they don't harbor bitter feelings. How many times have you heard a friend or family member lament their unfortunate position? Typically, the person has found a job on Monster.com, the newspaper, or heard of it from a friend. This "golden" position is just perfect. The person is qualified, the job is in a great growing company, and it pays significantly more!

However, instead of applying for the job the person simply sulks around the office lamenting his or her unfortunate position and the low under-market salary. The effects of this impression can manifest themselves in many ways. Employees feel they don't have to try as hard, work as long, or do as much. When they are up-front about why they are upset, you actually have an advantage. You can make them understand the current market or they will choose to work harder or to leave the organization. No matter what happens, the problem is resolved quickly.

When employees don't say anything and simply feel underpaid and underappreciated, it can be worse. You can be in the position of not knowing where performance issues are coming from. One manager told us about an employee she "inherited" from her old boss. It was a very odd situation. No matter what task the employee was given, or what goal he was asked to complete, he seemed unable to understand the instructions or complete the tasks. A month or two later, the company had across-the-board layoffs and of course the manager picked this employee to fire. It was only after the individual left that the manager found out the cause of the performance problems. It turned out that the employee was unhappy with his new manager and his position and was actively trying to be difficult. Although this employee never said a word to his manager that there was a problem, the effect of his passive-aggressive behavior was damaging to the company.

Therefore, it is important to take proactive steps to ensure that you are aware of, and on top of, the employee morale. The more conscious you are of the situation, the better your chances of fixing a problem before it becomes an issue.

3.1 Conduct regular performance reviews

One of the ways to ensure that you aren't the victim of internal sabotage is to conduct regular performance reviews. Although it may take a few hours per person to complete, the benefits are often worth the time. To start your own internal reviews, you can follow these simple steps:

- Document each job. In order to ensure that both you and your employees understand the requirements of the job, take a few moments and write a job description. This will be valuable for employee reviews and to ensure that processes listed are fully documented. Also, if the employee ever leaves, you will be able to quickly post for a replacement.

- Set standards. For each part of the job, set standards that you want the employee to achieve. Do the tasks have to be completed on a daily basis? Is there any way to measure the results? Are there any consequences of poor performance? Establishing these items up front will let you have more control over what is done, when it is done, and how it is done. Then, present these to the employees before the start of the review period. This will ensure that they have sufficient time for feedback and therefore, buy-in.

Moneymaker: By relating each employee's work directly to the bottom line, the employees will understand how they contribute to the growth and success of the company. Tying each employee's objectives to goals that are profitable for the business will also ensure that your employees are focused on growing the company and not just completing a task.

- Designate a regular review period. Choose how often you intend to provide your employees with regular feedback. Is it every six months from their hire date? (This may become difficult to remember.) Or is it once a year at the same time every year? Whatever you choose to do, make sure the employees understand the time frame you will be using. Also, tie raises and bonuses to this period. This will generally prevent unexpected salary conversations during the year.

- Document manager's comments. Make sure that your review process is not so form-oriented that it doesn't allow your comments. Having a section dedicated to your comments or the individual manager's comments is an important part of any review.

3.2 Provide constructive feedback

In order for a review to be valuable to both you and the employee, you must ensure that it only contains constructive feedback. This is not the same as positive feedback. Constructive feedback is information that is presented in such a way that it can be useful for the employee's personal growth. This may mean reminding the employee of past successes and recommending that he or she continues to work in the same way.

It can also mean identifying key weaknesses and outlining steps that will allow the person to be more successful in these areas. In both cases, the feedback should be clear, to the point, and concrete.

3.2a Be honest

Reviews should not simply be a time for a pep talk, but must be an honest evaluation of the individual's strengths and weaknesses. Make sure to be honest about the individual's performance. Do not provide praise in mediocre areas. If you are not honest during the review process, the employees will stop taking reviews seriously. Getting praise when it isn't warranted is as disheartening as getting complaints for a job that was well done. Both ways, the employee is not being recognized and the feedback will fall on deaf ears.

3.2b Document strengths as well as weaknesses

Within your document make sure to highlight areas of success as well as areas of weakness. Pick one or two areas in each category. Ideally the strengths should represent those characteristics that you want the employee to continue showing and the weaknesses should be those areas you would like the person to work on in the future.

Lifesaver: For a candid view of your employees, solicit feedback from your customers or clients. When we started doing this with our employees, we were surprised at the feedback we received. Some of our best technical resources received terrible customer reviews. As a small-business owner, knowing your customers' impression of your employees is an important part of ensuring high-quality customer service.

3.2c Use examples and consequences

When you can, make sure to use concrete examples to prove your points. The more specific your feedback, the better it will be received. For example, saying, "You are always late," while true, isn't constructive. Writing a more detailed explanation is more helpful. A better way of saying this would be to explain the specifics around the problem as well as the impact it had on the business. For example, "The employee has arrived late to open the store two out of the last four days he had that responsibility. As a result, the company has lost sales and experienced poor customer service."

3.2d Don't allow any surprises

Ideally, try to provide examples that have already been discussed with the employees. For instance, if you have consistently spoken with them about smiling when they are with customers and they have failed to improve in this area, you would want them to be aware, in writing, that this is having an impact on their performance. Having discussed and then written about this may reinforce the importance of this action. However, there is no reason to wait for a review. If a problem is significant enough, it should be discussed with the employee the moment it occurs or as soon after as is reasonable. Reviews should not replace day-to-day management or oversight.

3.2e Solicit employee comments

After you present the review, make sure to take some time to listen to the employee's feedback. Solicit it if necessary. Some questions you may want to ask to start a discussion include:

- Did you agree that these are your best strengths? If so, why? If not, what strengths would you have chosen?

- Did you agree that these are your weakest areas? What do you think you can do to improve your areas of weakness?

- Do you need anything from me as your manager to be more successful here?

- What opportunities do you see for growth? How do you see yourself growing in this company over the next year?

- Do you believe it is a fair assessment?

By the end of the conversation, you should be confident that the employee understood the review. He or she should be able to articulate the areas in which he or she is most successful. If the employee understands and values your feedback, these actions should continue. It is equally important, if not more important, to ensure that he or she understands the negative feedback as well. If you want the employee to grow in the areas that are a struggle, the employee must start by understanding the concerns.

At the end of the review, let the employee know what the next steps are. He or she needs to be accountable for improving in these areas. Your employee needs to do the work; you just need to point the way. If the employee isn't willing to work to keep his or her job, then you are under no obligation to keep it for the person.

 **Lifesaver:** Whenever any manager has problems with an employee, make sure to put the issue in writing. Ideally, present this document to the employee and have it signed. Having a problem documented will sometimes make the concern seem more concrete and if you wind up having to terminate the employee, this documentation will help you defend yourself in a wrongful termination suit.

4. Setting Level Employee Expectations

As a business owner, you should consider what type of employee perks you are willing to provide before your employees bring it to your attention. If you haven't decided for yourself what types of benefits you will offer, you may find yourself struggling to answer your employees' questions. Instead, identify the cost of the benefits, and estimate how much you will spend. Also make sure your business will be able to afford these costs. There are two main times when you will need to communicate these benefits to your employees:

1. As part of their regular review. Take the time to let them know if the company is on track to meet its financial goals. Talk through any benefits that you will be adding or removing in response to the company's current revenue. Also, be prepared to communicate the company vision as well as the subgoals that they can complete to help you reach these goals. If you aren't giving raises, be upfront and honest about that as well. Taking this time to discuss your employees' financial compensation and rewards will help prevent employee discontent later.

2. During hiring conversations. If your company normally provides additional benefits, make sure to mention it during the hiring process so that potential employees can understand the full terms of their compensation package. By clearly outlining these items, you can ensure there are no hurt feelings and misunderstandings later on.

For instance, some companies provide yearly bonuses. Instead of telling your employees at a random point in the year that you think they will get a bonus, try to be more specific and make sure that these benefits are tied to the success of the company. If you simply state that you would like to be able to give the employees a 10 percent bonus, this could be an issue if the company is not as profitable as you expected. However, if you say that the employees will get a 10 percent bonus if you exceed your company's sales goals by 10 percent, you have given the employees something to strive for. This reward is both specific and achievable. Plus, the employees can all help achieve this goal and if it is not met, immediately understand why you cannot provide the bonuses you had hoped to give. Once you determine what you will offer, make sure to take the time to document it in simple, easy-to-understand terms.

12

DOCUMENT YOUR CRITICAL PROCESSES TO ENSURE CONSISTENT, QUALITY CUSTOMER SERVICE

Unexamined processes can lead to catastrophic excesses. Businesses simply don't have the luxury of waste anymore. Whether it's wasting time, effort, money, or resources, those days are gone. If you want your business to survive recessions, it's critical to pay close attention to how you conduct your business and not just assume that everything is going well. This means auditing and re-examining the way your company works.

It is much easier to prevent mistakes than to resolve them after they have happened. Employees may not even know there is a problem. For example, one help desk number we heard about had significant issues in this area. Every time a customer called in, he or she would receive a different answer. Soon, the communal advice said that customers should simply keep calling back until they found a customer service representative whose answer they liked! As a result, the business had numerous unnecessary support calls, an increase in dissatisfied customers, and an embarrassing reputation.

By documenting the process and implementing rigid controls around your most critical functions, you can ensure that problems like these don't occur. Even office or technical functions can benefit from having formal documentation. Very often, this documentation helps make sure that employees are consistently meeting customer expectations and providing quality service. Further, by having critical processes documented there is now a fair way to audit the work and guarantee that customers are receiving the high-quality service they deserve.

Lifesaver: If most of your company's functions are conducted on computers, you may want to make your forms electronic instead of paper. Electronic forms can be created with applications such as Microsoft Word or Microsoft Excel or it is possible to purchase more elaborate applications that will track when each task is executed and by whom.

1. The Benefits of Documents and Processes

Creating documents will take time and effort on the part of you and your team. In fact, some employees will probably resist investing their time in this project. Therefore, it is important that you convey to your team why you want them to participate in this activity and just how they, the business, and your customers will benefit. Of course, while it's helpful to explain, at the end your employees work for you and your orders must be carried out.

One of the most obvious ways to use these documents is to reduce the overhead associated with bringing on new employees. Whenever you have new employees come on board, chances are that you have to mentor them and train them in common everyday tasks. In some cases, this could mean asking the new employee to remember and correctly execute a long series of complex tasks. This means that the employees typically will take longer to get up to speed and may make mistakes at first that have to be corrected by other, more experienced staff. Having forms to use can take the place of this cumbersome exercise. If the form is clear and easy to use, it reduces the amount of time training takes, and increases quality from the new person.

Another benefit is that processes and forms allow experienced employees to share their knowledge without spending hours on instruction. In our company, we use forms for all common yet complex computer repairs. Repairs such as spyware and virus removal typically need to be completed over the course of few days, so the forms allow multiple employees to work on one machine with confidence. The form standardizes the work that needs to be completed, and since each step has a sign-off box, the employees are confident that they are each completing the "next step" that is necessary for the repair to be successful.

Forms and process documents also ensure that the customer is getting a consistent experience, especially for service offerings. Even though all your employees work for your company, they may not agree on the "best" way to conduct business. When you create your forms and processes you will probably be surprised to learn just how much variation exists in your organization. By taking the time to document best practices, you can be assured that each employee has completed the work to your company's standards. Sometimes, this change is so significant that you will immediately see a decline in customer complaints as well.

With all of the efficiencies that forms and processes can bring to an organization, your employees will also benefit. They will be able to complete tasks faster, with less concern that they are making mistakes. Plus, with fewer training issues and customer complaints to deal with, there will also be reduced interruptions and stress.

If you have documents and processes in place, you will have an easier time replicating your company's success when you expand. These documents can be taken directly to the next office or location and used to get that new location up and running quickly. Further, if you were to consider franchising instead of opening another office yourself, this documentation could be the beginning of your franchise documents.

When we implemented this in our business, we saw dramatic, profitable changes. For us, our first priority as a retail store was to ensure quality service. This meant that each team member was following the best practices possible. When we first bought the business, our store manager personally assured us that processes were completed correctly. However, without a fully documented process, we found customers were complaining about poor quality, employees were not sure what tasks were to be completed for each repair, and our manager was heavily involved in checking each computer personally.

It didn't take long to realize that the business was not running as efficiently as possible. We listed the most common and complex processes and started documenting. It took almost a month to get each process properly documented and then about two months for the team to reliably fill out all the newly created forms. During this period we had to constantly measure our results to ensure that we were making the right changes. However, in just two short months the store saw reduced customer complaints, faster turnaround time on customer orders, and increased profits — all without an increase in overhead.

2. Picking the Right Processes to Document

When you are trying to ensure quality customer service, it is helpful to document what you do and how you do it. However, you don't want to document everything you do. Only those items that meet the following criteria should be documented:

- The process must be critical to your business. For instance, if signing up a new customer is critical to your business, you should outline what this process entails. You definitely don't need a process for trivial, obvious tasks such as emptying the trash.

- The process shouldn't be documented anywhere else. This means that if you are using a standard software program such as MS Office, you should not document how to use this product as there are "help features" and tutorials that should be used instead.

- The process should not document a government regulation or government process. Since these may change over time, it is risky to document these legal procedures in your own training manual. Employees are liable to rely on this information instead of staying up-to-date with current local laws.

Once you get your list together of critical items, try to narrow it down to the top five. These items can be documented first to give your company experience with this process and to ensure that it adds value to your organization.

> # WARNING:
> Do not give your employees or others copies of your process documents or forms. These documents contain your company's best practices and should be considered confidential, proprietary information. You may even want the footer of each document to display your company name and the phrase "Confidential — For Internal Use Only."

After you have selected the processes you want to document, start by asking the employee who is most proficient at completing this task to document what he or she does and why. Have the employee do it in much the same way he or she would if he or she was training a new employee on the process. This means fully dissecting and describing each process. A standard process document should generally include the following sections:

- Purpose: Detail what is being documented and why.

- Audience: Who should typically be using the document.

- Steps: List of what needs to be completed.

- Controls: List of what items are checked or audited by a manager, customer, or coworker.

- Date and history: Always include the date the process was created as well as a brief history of any updates that were made to the document and by whom.

3. Designing Forms That Save Time

Before you can think about how to create a form, you should decide what forms you will create. A good rule to use is that you only need a form if the task spans a great deal of time (i.e., takes many hours or days), has numerous steps, or is completed by multiple employees. In other words, do not use forms when they will add more work than value.

When you design forms that are going to be used regularly by your employees, you want them to be as easy to use as possible. Too often, people create forms that are long, arduous, confusing, and time consuming. The purpose of the form is not to make the employee's life more difficult! Forms should always make the task easier and faster! There are a few simple rules that need to be followed to create forms that save time and add efficiency:

- Limit the length: This may be the most important step. Forms used on a daily basis should be no more than one page if possible — the shorter the form the better.

- Summarize information, don't add details: Forms should be used to add efficiency, not to act as a training manual for inexperienced employees. You should be able to use the jargon of your trade on your forms. Your employees should be experienced enough to understand these terms. For instance, on our repair forms, we may write "reboot" since any computer technician would understand what needs to be done. However, a training manual may be more detailed and may even contain a page outlining how to perform a computer reboot.

- Outline the critical steps: If individual steps are completed, they should be outlined clearly on the form and numbered to indicate that these things should be performed in order. Do not number items that do not need to be performed in order.

- Include the goal: Avoid the temptation to use more than one form for multiple functions. Each form should have one goal that will be completed.

- Include check boxes: Each step or item that needs to be completed should have a checkbox so that it is easy to track.

- Require employee sign off: If the form will be completed by only one person, you can include a sign-off space for the employee to confirm that the form was completed. If multiple employees are completing one form, then do not include a sign-off. Instead, each step should have a line for the employees to initial as it is completed.

- Include audit fields: At the end of the form, include an audit line. This will remind employees that these forms may be checked and when the form is reviewed will provide an easy way of documenting that the review was properly completed.

A well-designed form will actually make the task faster to complete than it was before. Therefore, the best way to tell if you have achieved this goal is to test the form. Have an experienced employee try to complete the standard process using the form that has been created. If this form makes the job faster, it is successful. If it is ambiguous, has steps out of order, or has any other problems, correct it and try again. The form isn't complete until it adds efficiency to the existing process.

 **Lifesaver:** As each document is completed, have the entire team review the document and add their ideas. By having the entire group review each document, you will ensure that the best ideas are incorporated into the process. Further, since each team member has had the opportunity to contribute to building the process, they will be more committed to completing it as designed.

4. Measure What Matters

If you are serious about ensuring a great customer experience, you want to anticipate problems before a customer brings them to your attention. The best way to identify poor customer service is to have methods to find it yourself. Forms and processes can help give you this capability. Take some time (or have your senior employees take some time) to audit a sample of the forms that were recently completed. Make sure that the sample is representative. That means that the sample must include forms completed by various employees for different customers.

Then, ensure the required tasks were completed. This means reviewing the work completed against the appropriate forms and processes. Any mistakes should be noted and discussed with the employees individually. This will make them understand that you are serious about customer service and making sure the customer has a great, consistent experience. Just be careful not to take process implementation too far. For example, a store in our area fired an entire department after it was determined they had gone outside of process a handful of times. While that may have been justified, such drastic actions should really be restricted to unethical employees rather than affecting the entire department.

5. Regular Reviews

As with anything else that is critical to your business, all process documents and forms should be reviewed regularly to ensure that they are not out of date. Sometimes even your best employees will stop using the forms when they are no longer relevant but won't bring it to your attention. Have your senior employees sign off on each form and process document at least once a quarter to ensure they are being kept up and that any required changes are made.

13

TRAIN YOUR EMPLOYEES TO INCREASE SALES AND IMPROVE PROFITABILITY

Any store owner will tell you that successful sales are the cornerstone of the business. Unfortunately, what many businesses find is that instead of having sales achieved by all members of the organization, there are only a few people who bring in the bulk of the revenue. Everyone has to work to the best of their ability or the entire company suffers. A small business owner, especially in a fiscally tight economy, cannot afford to have only one or two people who can sell the products. Instead, the owner of a business needs his or her entire staff to be focused on making sales.

1. Sales and Satisfied Customers

All businesses want to have satisfied customers. For most owners this is the ultimate goal of their business — to help an individual fill a need in a way that adds value to his or her life. However, sometimes store employees,

and even store owners, forget there cannot be "satisfied customers" if the patrons leave the store without ever buying anything! They have to be "customers" first before they can ever be "satisfied customers"! Although this may seem obvious to you, the store owner, it may not be obvious to your employees.

At Arizona Computer Outlets, we ran into this problem once. Our store offers everyone a "free 15-minute in-store diagnostic" for any computer problem. This is a strong competitive advantage that allows us to bring new customers in the store (most of our competitors provide this service for a hefty fee). Further, we encourage our technicians to be honest with the customers even if it means telling them that their computer is fine and no service is required. In general, about 30 percent of our in-store diagnostics result in the customer choosing not to repair his or her machine, either because the computer is fine or because they don't feel it is worth the cost. Some of these result in new computer sales, but the "free" diagnostic really is "free" and with no obligation, so some of these shoppers leave the store with nothing. However, after owning the business for a few months, we found that this number was increasing rapidly. Soon more than 60 percent of all customers that received a diagnostic were never completing any service or buying any new items. As owners, we didn't realize the significance of this until one loyal customer finally called and complained. Her exact words were, "What do I have to do to be able to buy a new computer from you?" At that moment, we found a problem that some small-business owners face and often don't realize — employees that believe they shouldn't sell, to make the customers happy.

After speaking with the customer we found that she had been in numerous times to have her computer checked. Her main complaint was her computer was just too slow. When the technicians looked at it they only offered her a free tune-up (a standard part of our warranty). Despite the fact that this did improve her performance, she still wasn't satisfied and came back. During her next visit, since the computer was very old, they offered to replace some of her computer's parts with used parts to improve the speed. Disliking the idea of having used parts, she turned the offer down and left again as they suggested no other options.

All she wanted was a brand new, fast computer and was upset that they never suggested that she get one. However, when we talked with the technicians, they had a different impression. To them she was an older woman who they assumed was on a fixed income and who would not want to spend money on a new computer. They judged her on her appearance and never investigated her needs. In this case, the employees failed basic customer service. By not even showing her a new computer and only offering less expensive solutions, they did not meet her needs. She left unhappy and if she hadn't had a strong relationship with the store, she probably would not have returned. After talking with numerous business owners and employees alike, there are a few main sales myths that seem to prevent people from closing the sale.

1.1 Sales myth 1: Our products are too expensive

Price does not always indicate value and the most successful business is not always the one with the least expensive product. In every business type, there are successful companies with low-cost products as well as successful companies with very pricey products. In most cases, these types of products do not even compete! For instance, Burger King is well known for its fast service and low-cost food. The cost of a full meal (i.e., burger, soda, fries, and a dessert) is typically less than $10. Smith & Wollensky is known for their high-end steak dinners and a full meal (i.e., four wines paired with five courses including a dry-aged sirloin entrée) currently sells for over $100. Of course, in both cases, the customers choose the product because they believe they are getting value.

On the one hand, when customers go to Burger King, they are choosing speed, convenience, and low cost. They are comfortable with using plastic knives and forks, filling their own sodas, and finding their own table. The meal itself is a "good value." On the other hand, the very same customers would have a very different view of value if they were provided a Whopper in the same location for over $100! In this price range, Smith & Wollensky knows how to provide that value. The ambiance of the restaurant, from the crisp tablecloths to the long, five-course meal is all expected for that amount of money.

In both cases, it isn't the price that is driving the customers' decision to purchase the product, but the value they receive from the product. Customers always want good value. Customers will only decide a product is a good value if they feel that they will receive good measure for their money. This does not mean that your products must be the cheapest. The services that come with the product, the convenience of the purchase, or the status associated with the purchase are all reasons why customers may buy from you, which it is because of the perceived value, not the lowest price.

Make sure all of your employees understand the value of your product. If you are trying to be the low-cost provider, give them information about your competitors' prices, and make sure they understand how much lower your prices really are. If you are the high-quality provider, make sure that each person on your staff can explain why your products are of higher quality than the competition. Whichever way your product adds value to the customer should be understood by all the employees on your staff. If necessary, call a team meeting to discuss these ideas as a group and to ensure that everyone has the same understanding.

1.2 Sales myth 2: I'm not in the sales department

All employees in any business are in sales. When a customer interacts with any employee, they don't consider the employee's role. They simply see the employee as a representative of the business. Therefore, the impression that the employee gives the customer is important. For instance, one large department store in our area is great at sales. People are available and easy to work with. However, returning a product is a different experience. There is only one area where you can make returns and the employees are not friendly. Unfortunately, even one bad experience can sour a customer on a business. To the customer, it doesn't matter if the employee is in sales or not, what matters is that the employee is a representative of the business and at that moment, that employee is directly in charge of the customer's sales experience.

Whenever any employee is dealing with a customer, in any circumstance, the employee must understand that for that moment, the customer is the "boss" since customers pay the bills and their salaries! Each customer must be treated with respect and while a customer may become curt, abrupt, or dissatisfied, it is never appropriate for any employee in any department to respond in kind. As a representative of the business, each employee must treat all customers with respect, understanding, and patience no matter what department that employee works in. While he or she may not be directly selling a product, in the end, every employee represents your company's brand and each employee can harm sales directly with a poor attitude.

Lifesaver: In general, any employee who answers a phone should always be smiling when greeting a caller. Although the person on the other end of the phone can't see a smile, the emotion comes through loud and clear. Remember, even though the patron isn't physically in the store, each customer still deserves to be treated in a friendly manner. Smiling while on the phone should be common practice for all of your employees in all departments.

1.3 Sales myth 3: That customer can't afford it

Never, ever judge a customer by his or her appearance. This has been said many times, but it is always true. Almost every business owner can tell the story of the "big fish" customer that they didn't expect, which is that the customer walked in and the owner never believed that the individual would spend any money, let alone the large dollars that the person did. For instance, while many people might think that a computer store shopper may typically be a teenager looking to do some online gaming, a more typical patron at our store is an older woman who wants to receive emails from her granddaughter. This is because many young gamers build their own computers, whereas older customers often don't want the hassle. Of course, this is not always true. Not all customers will look the same or act the same and while some salespeople will "swear" to you that they can size up a customer, as a business owner, you are looking for profitable customers, not customers that fit a particular stereotype.

All of your employees must understand that each person who walks into your store is a potential customer and each customer must be treated with respect and the assumption that he or she will be a great customer. It is up to the customer to decide what he or she can afford, not the store staff.

Of course, as a business owner, you want to make sure your employees understand that any type of discrimination can have very significant consequences for both the employee and the company. The bad press from even the perception that a company may not be treating all customers fairly is a huge problem for a business owner, especially a small-business owner. Any negative publicity for a small business could cause the business sales to drop dramatically and sometimes even cause a business to close.

1.4 Sales myth 4: That customer doesn't need it

Hardly anyone could make an argument that potato chips are ever really "needed" and yet there are entire companies dedicated to the production of this tasty, if nutritionally questionable, food. As a business owner, you may offer services that your employees themselves don't value or understand. For instance, there is a pet-boarding service that not only boards pets, but also provides owners with a wide variety of options for purchase. Owners can purchase special playtime for their pets, treats, and even special meals. While many people may not understand the value of these services, to dog lovers, it is hard not to purchase all of these treats for their beloved Fido!

Make sure that you regularly cover the services your business offers with each of your employees. Before you add a new service, let your employees know why you think it is valuable and what type of customer will value the new service most. Even if the employees don't have a personal need for your services, they should be able to offer these items to a potential customer with enthusiasm and confidence.

Lifesaver: To determine how your employees treat customers, you may want to have a friend visit your store as a "secret shopper." You can keep it simple and have the individual purchase a product, or make it more difficult and have your friend come in with a complaint. If you have a camera system, watch what happens. If not, then simply get your friend's feedback. The experience will help you coach your staff to more effectively serve your customers.

1.5 Sales myth 5: We haven't had a serious buyer all day

The truth is that most individuals that make the effort to go to the store are actually looking to purchase either a service or a product — if he or she feels it is a good value. Unfortunately, most customers won't tell you why they are leaving without making a purchase. This makes it easy to conclude that a customer was never interested in the first place. How many times have you yourself said that you were "just browsing" and then purchased from another store instead? In truth, very few people enjoy wasting their time.

When someone walks into your store, he or she should be considered a serious buyer. Giving up on a sale before someone even speaks with the customer is probably one of the most damaging sales myths that exist! The propagation of this belief can often cause morale issues and in turn reduce sales. Even if the customer does not choose to purchase, he or she may still become a customer. Having a great experience when you walk into a store may make the difference between a casual shopper and a lifelong, dedicated customer. Just a few suites down from our computer store is a tire company. Every once in a while, we get customers who wander into our store "browsing" while they wait for their tires to get changed. However, the fact they came in at all tells you that they are interested in computers or technology.

As an owner, excuses of any sort cannot be allowed when it comes to sales. Employees that repeat defeatist phrases can often infect the morale of your entire staff. Deal with each of these items as individual problems to ensure that they don't spread. If you hear anyone complaining in this way or making similar statements about how "impossible" it is to make a sale, make sure to take him or her aside and ameliorate any concerns. If that is ineffective, you may even have to take more extreme actions to ensure that such an attitude doesn't spread throughout your store or to your customers.

Moneymaker: When a customer leaves your business without making a purchase, make sure that he or she leaves happy. Smile as you say, "Come again" and if you can, provide the person with either a business card or a brochure. Sometimes, these little items will bring customers back to your store days or even weeks later to purchase a product.

1.6 Sales myth 6: Customers just don't like salespeople

Customers don't mind salespeople; what most people don't like is being "sold." Most people don't visit stores because they want to be convinced to buy a product; most people visit a store because they are trying to solve a problem. The problem can take many forms. For example, when someone walks into a travel agency, he or she may be looking for a fun-filled family getaway or he or she may be looking for a romantic private retreat. Either way, it is important to understand the customer's needs if you want to be successful at sales. While you could just try to push the cruise with the highest margin, in the long run you will make more by selling the vacation the person will enjoy best.

Discuss with your employees the importance of providing solutions and not "selling" products. Very often people trying to sell products spend a great deal of the time talking *at* the customer. Instead of trying to inundate the customer with facts and figures, try to spend some time asking questions and understanding the customer's perspective. Have your employees practice talking with customers to determine customer needs and make sure they are all aware of the strengths and benefits of your bestselling items. If your employees don't understand these items, or believe in the products, odds are they won't be very effective at selling.

A great book to help people learn the difference between pushing a product and selling a solution is *Solution Selling: Creating Buyers in Difficult Selling Markets*, by Michael T. Bosworth (McGraw-Hill, 1994). This book shows how focusing on solving the customer's problem can actually create more sales than just pushing a product.

1.7 Sales myth 7: Sales is just a numbers game

Part of the reason this myth is alive and well is because of how varied customers are. On the one hand, some customers are loyal to a brand or a store. When they walk in they know what they want and will buy it even if they are dealing with a difficult employee. On the other hand, some individuals truly are just window shopping and wouldn't buy the product if it were 90 percent off and delivered for free! This type of customer variety may cause people to assume that with enough volume, anyone could be successful. While that may be true, the typical business cannot generate an infinite volume of potential customers.

This is especially true for non-retail businesses that rely on proposals or cold calling to get new customers. While it is possible to simply "call everyone," it is better to target your customers before you even begin to approach them. Identify who your potential customers are and why they would benefit from your business. This will allow a much more focused approach to getting their business. For example,

there was a company that sold security cameras to nearby businesses. This group would target a type of company by using the Yellow Pages and then build their scripts for that company. If they were looking at selling to beauty salons, their tactics would be different then when they were selling to gas stations. Even though they were using a basically free general lead list, by focusing the company's products and communication it was more effective than when it tried more limited lead lists.

2. Look for Sales Opportunities

Before you start trying to get new customers, take a look at the individuals that are currently visiting your business. Chances are you have spent good money on advertising to bring people to your business; however, those dollars are all wasted if the deal can't be closed and the customer walks out. Each individual that walks into your store, calls your number, or agrees to a sales call is an opportunity. Unless your business boasts 100 percent customer conversion rates (i.e., the ability to turn a new interested individual into a customer), your business has a significant opportunity to increase sales. Therefore, the very first place to look for sales opportunities is within your business.

To begin you have to take an honest look at each individual that comes in contact with your business. Start by watching a typical day. How many people walk into your store? Of those that enter your establishment, what percentage actually buys something? For each person that doesn't make a purchase, talk with your employees and try to determine why the person left. If you have a courteous staff that has greeted each customer who has entered your store, asked the customers if they needed assistance, and in general tried to satisfy the customers' needs, you may find more opportunities than you think! Were the customers looking for a product you don't carry? Or perhaps a size that was out of stock? Could it have been ordered or arranged? By talking about these losses with your staff you may find new business opportunities, product lines, or a better understanding of your customer.

Moneymaker: At the end of every "failed" sales call, have the salespeople complete a postmortem sales document. This document should include information about whom they spoke with, what the customer's objections were, and why the sale didn't work out. Sharing this information among your staff will allow your people to share ideas for overcoming these objections and help them tune their presentations to make the next sale.

Of course, it is possible that your staff will have no idea why the customer left. In this case you may want to review your customer service. Did anyone speak with the individual? Or did your advertising dollars go to waste as your employees ignored a potential sale? Remember, each individual that walks out of your store without a purchase, or rejects your salesperson without a contract, should be treated as an important loss that needs to be researched. It is important to learn from each lost sale so that you can strengthen the sales you have and expand your business to increase sale volume.

At the end of the day you may want to talk about these losses with your team. Was there anything they could have done differently? What other phrases or suggestions could they use the next time a similar situation occurs? With enough trial and error you will eventually see patterns in your business. Are there concerns customers have that they hesitate to mention? If so, your staff can learn to bring up these items themselves. Are there product benefits that should be mentioned up front? Your team can construct small advertising signs that could sit in front of the product to ensure that both the customers and employees are aware of the benefits. Are there "deal breakers" that seem to come up frequently? If so, it may be possible to remediate or eliminate these problems before they kill a potential sale.

3. The Right Products to Up-Sell

Once you make a sale, you know the customer is comfortable with your business. To increase your sales, see what other types of products your customers may be interested in buying from you. For instance, when you order at McDonald's, the cashier commonly asks, "Do you want fries with that?" This seemingly simple question generates additional money for the restaurant each time a customer says "yes." Of course, it may not be this simple in your business. That doesn't mean that it will not be as lucrative.

Think about what your company sells most frequently and what you can up-sell on each order. Remember, the products that you up-sell should vary depending on what the customer has just purchased. Consider the following questions when choosing a product to up-sell:

- Does this up-sell product complement or relate well to what the customer just bought?

- Is the cost of the up-sell product significantly less than the product itself?

- Can the up-sell product help extend the life of the product that the customer just bought?

- Are you sure the customer can use the up-sell product?
- Does the up-sell product improve the original purchase?

When you are doing this exercise it may help to start by making a list of the more expensive products your business sells regularly. While it is possible to up-sell on less expensive products and sales, it is generally easier to add a small item to a large sale. Therefore, choose about five of your big-ticket items and identify one or two items that your employees can up-sell at the time of purchase. Remember to keep the list short to start — you can add more items as your staff become more comfortable with the products and more successful up selling. For example, the up-sell list at our computer store was relatively simple to start (see Sample 4).

Give your list of up-sell items to each of your employees and, if possible, post it on a private message board out of sight of the customers. Before you ask the employees to start up-selling, meet with the team and be sure that they know the up-sell products well. They should be able to discuss the benefits of the up-sell products and their relationship to the original main item. Ask a few questions to ensure that they can answer basic customer queries. If necessary, you can even have them practice role-playing to learn how to approach the up-sell.

Moneymaker: Make sure your impulse purchases are at an impulse price. For most businesses, this will mean placing small items by the register that are less than $5. For some stores, higher price points may be acceptable. Of course, make sure these items are clearly priced and labeled. You don't want to lose a sale because the customer didn't think the product was in his or her price range!

3.1 The right time to up-sell

If you want to successfully up-sell your customers, the best time to do so is after they have decided to purchase the main product and before they have had a chance to finalize the sale. Also, since this is just an up-sell — remember, you don't want the customer to change his or her mind about the main sale — it should be approached in a low-pressure manner.

One salon owner found a great time to up-sell to his customers. Whenever someone is getting his or her hair colored, while the customer is waiting for the color to set, the owner asks the person if he or she has a conditioner for color-treated hair. If the customer doesn't, he explains the benefits of using a shampoo and conditioner for color-treated hair and offers to sell the customer one of the products from his salon. Since the customer is waiting

SAMPLE 4
UP-SELL POSSIBILITIES

Main Product	Up-Sell Possibilities
Laptop	• Two- or three-year warranty • Spare laptop battery
Spyware removal	• Anti-virus and anti-spyware software
Computer tune-up	• Additional RAM upgrade

around anyway, this is a perfect time to try to up-sell the customer on a product that can help the person benefit from a service he or she is currently receiving! If the customer is interested, the owner then personally gets the shampoo and conditioner and gives it to the colorist to ensure it is not forgotten when the customer leaves the store.

Many businesses have this type of down-time sometime between the close of the sale and the scan of the credit card. Even if it is only the few moments while the person is waiting to complete his or her order, taking that time to talk about a related product or service provides a significant opportunity. If only 1 in every 20 customers chooses to purchase the additional products, the profit those sales generate has cost you almost nothing to obtain. Further, this simple act of up-selling to the customer not only makes the store more money but it is of benefit to the customer. If the store employees hadn't taken the time to make the customer aware of this product, the customer would never have had the opportunity to enjoy it.

4. Everything Should Be for Sale!

Now that you have been thinking about what products you want to carry, you can also start to think of what else you have available that you can sell or resell. For instance, our computer store often uses paper for the printer. Although paper is not "technically" a computer product, it can be considered an ancillary product for printers. Since we have shelf space available, we can sell paper as well! Even if it doesn't sell well, it is something we have to purchase anyway, so there is no harm done and there is potential for more sales.

If you have a store that services customers, make sure that your customers can buy the products you are using for them. For instance,

ensure at a hair salon that the shampoos and conditioners your stylists use are available to the customer. At a tanning salon, you can sell tanning lotions and other items.

There are a few warnings about selling products that you use in your business; first, all the products you are reselling should be labeled for resale. Second, be careful of sales-tax laws. Typically, when you purchase products for inventory you do not pay sales tax on the purchase as the products are for resale. However, when you purchase products for your office, you will have to pay sales tax since you are typically the consumer. Therefore, if you choose to sell any products that were purchased as office supplies, your inventory costs will probably be higher than normal. If these products turn out to be big sellers, you may want to start making two separate orders, one for your use as the customer (i.e., you pay the sales tax) and another for your inventory (i.e., you can use your reseller's license to purchase the product without paying the sales tax). Just remember to keep the quantities separated in your tracking system. If you aren't sure exactly how to do this or what the rules are in your state or province, contact an experienced accountant or bookkeeper for more information.

Moneymaker: In some businesses, vending machines can be very lucrative. If your store has traffic that includes children, small vending machines with balls, candy, or other items can be a new source of revenue. Customers of all ages can enjoy soda and snack vending machines as well. You can purchase and manage your own vending machines or you can contact a vending machine company that can handle management for you.

---

5. Taking Sales to the Next Level

Once you have finished these simple steps, it is time to take your sales to the next level. Each employee in your store is a member of the sales team, whatever their primary function. Therefore, as part of that team, they need to understand what selling is about and what their obligation is. Each person needs to know what it means to be in sales, what different types of sales styles look like, and how to improve their own style as much as possible. There are many different books on this topic, and you may want to read a few to find one that works best for you and your team.

A book that is easy to understand and that can help you immediately is *Sales Dogs: You Do Not Need to Be an Attack Dog to Be Successful in Sales*, by Blair Singer (Warner Business Books, 2001). This book outlines five different styles of selling as well as methods of coaching any of these styles. Using this book, you can effectively understand your employees' styles and your customers' needs.

14
TURN YOUR STORE INTO A SHOWPLACE SO YOU CAN ATTRACT NEW CUSTOMER DOLLARS

In this economy, you have to remove any impediment to your success, and that means doing all you can to look presentable. Most people would agree that a store that is clean and tidy will be more attractive to potential customers than one that appears unkempt and disheveled. Although we instinctively know this to be true, it isn't always easy to maintain a tidy appearance. At one point our computer store appeared so unkempt that the technicians complained that the store lacked space and customers very rarely browsed. However, our wake-up call didn't occur until one regular customer was truly surprised to learn we even sold computers! The following are some indicators that your store may be having an issue:

- Customers often ask for help finding your bestselling products.

- Your store has very few impulse purchases.

- You and your staff spend a significant amount of time during the day looking for inventory or parts.

- You rarely make ancillary sales when selling your most popular products.

- Inventory is off on small, easily-pocketed items that may have been stolen.

Each of these is a telltale sign of a store that has the opportunity to benefit from reorganization. With a minimum investment (and occasionally no investment at all), a small retail store can be totally transformed within days. For us, the entire planning stage took one week from start to finish. We then completed the changes during two business days and kept the store open. After we rearranged the store, the customers started browsing more and impulse purchases increased dramatically.

1. Transforming Your Store

A store transformation is not like redesigning a home. While most home redesign involves decorating, transforming a store should not be about color palettes or the latest trends. It is about making the customers comfortable in an environment that encourages them to make a purchase. This means your changes must be focused on inventory placement, customer impressions, and improving sales. Therefore, a store transformation does not start with appearances, but with an overall product review.

Before beginning a store transformation, take some time to look around and learn more about your inventory and determine your most popular products. Check your sales transactions and review your sales for the last six months. Pay special attention to the products that have sold frequently as well as the products that haven't. Before you begin to reorganize you should know what items —

- are your most popular sellers,
- are your most profitable sellers,
- draw your customers, and
- customers ask for.

 **Lifesaver:** If you aren't sure what your most popular product is or even how to rearrange the items, start by scouting your competitors. Visiting their shops will allow you to see how other stores are arranged, what items they sell, and how they are advertised before you make any changes to your own store. This will cost you very little and has the potential to save you a great deal of time and money.

Next, you will need to understand your customers. Watch your customers for a day or two at your store. When your customers enter your store, watch where they go and how they shop. Pay attention to the products that they notice and the ones they ask your staff to help them find. Consider the following questions as you observe your customers:

- When customers enter your store, where do they go?
- Is it easy for the customers to browse?
- Are the aisles too narrow? Or are they too wide (and can you afford to add more products)?
- Are the products organized in a way that makes it easy to find the items the customers are looking for?

Remember, the purpose of redesigning your store is not just to create a more *comfortable* customer environment; it is primarily to create a more *profitable* customer environment. Therefore, while a beautiful layout would be nice, the most important factor is to ensure that the product layout encourages the customers to purchase. To do this, your retail space must be maximized to allow more products and more opportunities for customers to purchase from you.

2. Creating the New Layout of Your Store

To start, document your old, current layout by simply using a pen and paper to draw it. Be sure to include all large objects such as racks, tables, and product stands. Once you have completed your drawing, consider how much of your space is used for selling customer products and how much is used for your office space, registers, and service. Ideally, the majority of your store should be dedicated to products if the majority of your income is from sales. Companies that are more service-oriented will need a higher portion of the store dedicated to a service area.

However, the decision must be justifiable based on your sales. Remember, the more space you have for product, the more opportunities for new sales.

Lifesaver: When redesigning your store, look for ways to reuse your current shelf hooks and tables rather than spending money on new items. If you have to choose between new purchases and reusing old parts, remember, the goal is to increase revenues, not your spending.

On your paper model, it will take only moments to test out new ideas and envision new layouts. Play with your design until you feel it optimizes the space in your store. Remember a few minutes in the planning stage can save hours of work. Changing your store without a documented layout can cause confusion and be time consuming, especially since odds are good that you will probably try multiple arrangements before you settle on the one that's the best for you. Feedback from friends, family, employees, and customers should be solicited and the results incorporated into the design.

3. Remember the Best Changes Are Free

The dramatic change to your store, which can add a remarkable improvement to your bottom line, can often be achieved at very low cost, (sometimes no cost) to the business. For most businesses, it is not necessary to move walls or change floor plans. Dramatic changes can be made by rearranging your existing products and shelving. The key is to remember the redesign is about improving sales, not increasing costs. Therefore, before you consider any new purchase, ensure you are making full use of your current items. All existing shelving, hangers, and displays should be used before you consider new purchases. When designing your store, keep the following design tips in mind:

- Get rid of damaged items: Tables that look worn out, chairs that are torn, and shelves that are dirty can ruin your customer impression. There are many inexpensive ways to prevent customers from seeing damaged items. Hiding the item, moving it to a little used area, or replacing it outright can help improve your customer image.

- Display short shelves and racks in the middle of the store: Placing shorter shelves (i.e., around three to four feet high) in the middle of the store will make the store appear more open since most customers can see over these items.

- Take advantage of wall space: With walls, you can take advantage of almost every inch of height. Using displays that travel up to the top of the wall may not always be easy to reach by a customer, but it can be an excellent place to display or even store new products. Whenever possible, take advantage of the wall space — even if it is with a simple ad or vendor poster.

- Consider moving registers to the front of the store: For most small businesses it is valuable to have a register near the front. This ensures that your customers are always greeted when they enter the store, even if your employees are helping another individual.

- Hide wiring and cords: For the safety of your customers you should always attempt to hide any wiring or cords that could trip someone in your store.

During your design transformation, the ideas that cost the least will have the most value. Do not be tempted to change too much or purchase new, unnecessary items. If you do find that you need to add any items, you may want to research low-cost alternatives. Hardware stores and discount stores sometimes have inexpensive shelving and cabinetry available. For higher-end items, used furniture stores or online auctions sometimes provide low-cost alternatives to buying new, expensive products.

4. Take Advantage of Professional Designers

Franchise owners may not have as much flexibility as individual owners to change their stores. However, if you're part of a franchise, you have the advantage of working with the parent company to get new ideas. Check out other local franchises and see what they do and how they do it. If there is none near you, ask the parent company to send you some photos of how their most successful franchises look. For instance, many franchises offer owners the ability to decorate with approved products created to highlight the company's products and services. These professionally designed products allow you to spend a limited investment on a professional product. Take advantage of these opportunities if you can.

For owners competing against a franchise, take advantage of the franchise's experience and design. Review the leading competitors in your area and determine which design elements you want to incorporate into your business. Obviously, you cannot use any trademarked or copyrighted materials, but layout ideas, such as types of fixtures, product placement, and sometimes decorations may be ideas that you can leverage to improve your business. Just make sure that you are never infringing on any proprietary materials.

5. Positioning Products in Your Store

When you consider where to place products, you should start by positioning your most popular products first. The items that are your biggest sellers should be in the most visible location for your customer. While this may be implemented differently for service businesses versus product stores, the idea is the same. Your customers need to see your most popular products.

5.1 Positioning popular products

Your most highly prized location in your store will include the space visible when you first enter the store. This space is viewable to all your customers and should display merchandise that are your most popular sellers. This will ensure that no customer can possibly miss the opportunity to make the purchase. Further, even if the customer is not looking for that product at that moment, making it easily available will let the person know that he or she can return to your store for it in the future.

After you position your most popular product, you can also add other popular products nearby. This can be critical as it creates an immediate impression of your store. If people walk in and immediately see products they like and are interested in buying, their impression of your store will be positive. If they walk in and immediately see products that are clearance items or other unpopular products, their impression will be based on those poor sellers instead. While there are great locations for popular products, there are also terrible locations. The back of the store is not a practical place for top sellers. Many customers will never travel to the back if they don't find things they like in the front.

Moneymaker: The most popular seller in any industry typically changes from year to year. Avoid letting old sales drive new product purchases by adding new items to your inventory regularly. Check your vendor catalogs quarterly for new products that fit your store. If you aren't sure what to add, call your vendors and ask them for a list of their best sellers. This list can serve as a good industry guide.

Another critical space is the area next to your register. This area is one which many of your customers see as they check out. While you will want to include some impulse purchases at the actual register, the area near the register is another good location for popular products.

You should also avoid cluttering your popular product area by adding too many slow sellers. If the area is overrun with unpopular items, then even the popular items will get lost in the mess.

5.2 Positioning popular products in your service business

You can be impacted by popular product positioning if you have a service-oriented business, such as a restaurant or a repair business. Check your price lists and menus. Are they easily showing your customers' favorite items? Are there too many items and services offered so that the most popular products can't be found? In some cases, changing your product's advertising, menus, or charge lists can increase sales by showing customers what you actually have to offer.

5.3 Product location increases impulse purchases

Every supermarket and large box store is a master of increasing impulse purchases. The most common rule of thumb is to ensure that candy bars, chewing gum, and breath mints can always be found next to the register. However, some well-thought-out stores take this a step further. Aside from small, unexpected purchases, think about including some items that your customers may want but forget. For example, some grocery stores keep milk in refrigerated coolers next to the registers; electronics stores keep batteries on the checkout counter; and beauty stores keep hair clips and shampoos within a few feet of a credit card machine. Each of these products represents the type of impulse purchase that fits each store.

Having impulse items easily available serves multiple purposes. It keeps your customers happy in that they find what they need, it keeps them from using your competitors (when they finally do remember what they needed), and it adds to your bottom line. Even if it results in an extra $10 in margin each week, you will earn more and your customers will be happier.

There are several ways to determine which impulse purchases are right for your business. First, you may want to review competing venues and see what they typically stock. Next, you may want to watch your customers or review your last six months of receipts. What small items that were less than $10 were most commonly purchased? These may be good indicators of products that fall into the impulse purchase category. If you really want to be sure what your customers want, remember to ask them. The standard query, "Have you found everything today?" Their answers will give you a wealth of information as well as an opportunity to make an additional sale.

6. Boost Sales by Offering New Ancillary Products

Every business has its popular sellers and then its moneymakers. The popular sellers are those items that customers come to your store to purchase. For instance, in a restaurant the popular seller may be the prime rib dinner. While these items draw customers to your business they may not always be the most profitable items your company sells. Often these items may carry some of the lowest margins in your store. However, the ancillary sales they generate may make selling the items more profitable. For instance, in fast food restaurants, sodas are often sold for up to $2 each although the actual cost of the soda is only a few cents. Ancillary purchases, such as drinks, alcohol, and other items make up for the lower-margin main courses. Each business has items that draw customers and items that are highly profitable. Therefore, it is important that each popular product be surrounded by its ancillary services. The same way no good food server would fail to offer the customer a drink, no small business should fail to offer its customers more profitable ancillary services.

First identify the ancillary items by reviewing what the company's best sellers are and then what other items customers purchase when they purchase these products. Each of these items that are related to the popular product should be identified and positioned near your most popular products. This means that while the popular product is immediately visible to the customer, these ancillary items may be located nearby. They could be on a shelf below the product, sitting next to the product, or on a shelf nearby. However, they must be visible to the customer and the sales staff when they are reviewing the popular product. This positioning will ensure that your sales staff remembers to offer the product to the customer and that the customer is able to easily obtain these items.

If you don't have enough related items and intend to expand your inventory, make sure that the new items fit in with your product line. Remember since these purchases are not planned, you are looking for items that meet a few criteria; they should be related to a most popular seller, they should be relatively inexpensive for the customer to purchase (i.e., about 10 to 20 percent of the price of the popular item), and they should be relatively high margin (i.e., 70 to 80 percent).

Moneymaker: In some cases ancillary products can be grouped together and sold to customers as an upgrade package. The group should be designed to meet the customers' needs and provide them a discount for the total purchase. For instance, when customer A purchases a used computer from our store, they also have the option of purchasing a used monitor, keyboard, and mouse package at a discounted rate.

7. Keep Your Customers Comfortable

When your customers enter your store or business they should feel comfortable with your establishment. The style of the store, the layout, and the design can all impact the customers' experience. Aside from the large changes, there are also smaller, simpler modifications that you can make that can quickly and easily make a customer more comfortable and therefore more likely to purchase.

7.1 Music

Music can make a difference to both your customers and your employees. It can impact the mood of the store quickly and significantly. Try to match your music with the impression your store is trying to make. For instance, heavy metal music, even if it is your favorite, has no place in an upscale jewelry store. However, in a downtown skateboard and helmet store, heavy metal music may be perfect for your typical customer. Just remember, the goal of the music is to make your customers comfortable so that they will be more likely to purchase from your store.

Keep in mind that the type of music that works for your customers may not be the style preferred by your staff. While you may try to find a compromise, in the end, it is about customer sales, not employee interests. To be sure you picked the type of music your customers like, ask them as they are at the register what they thought about your music. Eventually, this informal survey will help you choose a music style that is the best for your store. Of course, whatever music is selected, you should make sure that the music in your store is loud enough to be heard but soft enough so that it is not overwhelming.

Moneymaker: Add a new revenue stream by selling the music that is playing in your store. If you don't already work with a distributor that sells CDs, you can contact local artists for a low-cost option. Just make sure that the artists' style of music matches the image you want to create. Very often, new local artists will be excited to have the opportunity to be heard by your customers and have selling space in your store. You may not even have to pay anything for the initial few CDs if you agree to split profits on each sale!

7.2 Airflow and smells

Another ambient issue to consider is to make sure that the air in your location is always fresh and inviting. Some small businesses run in small locations with a few employees. In these confined quarters it is possible to get uninviting smells from time to time. Employee lunches, lack of airflow, cleaning supplies, and other, less savory items can sometimes make the store air seem stale at best, and smelly at worst. Make sure that your store is regularly aired out. If your employees eat in your store, it may need to be aired more frequently.

7.3 Temperature

For many shoppers and customers, the temperature of an establishment can also make a big difference. For instance, shops that sell clothing can often benefit from a fitting room temperature that is warm enough to make the customer comfortable enough to change. When pricing out the cost of this item, it may at first seem expensive and be tempting to ignore.

One restaurant we know attempted to save money by lowering the air conditioning during warm Arizona summers (which can reach 120 degrees Fahrenheit in July). While this energy efficient approach may have saved some money on the electric bill, it also lost them customers. The dining room, which connects to an open kitchen, became so unbearably hot that some customers asked to eat outside rather than inside! Therefore, before you change that dial, consider what your customers are doing at the store and what type of environment they expect. Your sales may depend on it.

8. Tots + Toys = Transactions!

Another consideration for your business is whether your typical customers are parents toting children. Most children do not have the interest or patience to shop with their parents (unless of course you run a toy store). As a result of the difficult tyke, many parents can feel rushed when they are shopping and try to complete all of their errands as quickly as possible. This leaves little time for browsing or impulse purchases. If you find that some of your customers are in this position, you may want to invest in a child-safe area of your store. Having a location where parents can deposit their children may make the parents more comfortable. Instead of them worrying that their children are destroying your store, they can relax and talk with your sales staff. That will give them the extra time to purchase what they really want.

This section does not have to be very large or specifically staffed. One clothing store for infants and toddlers has implemented this idea in a very easy and inexpensive way. In the middle of the merchandise and clothing, in the center of the store, are two small rectangular areas. One area is the register that is typically staffed by one or two store employees and the other area (toward the back of the store) is a child's play area. The play area is designed to entertain children, but not to be a day care. It is simply constructed of "walls" that are about three feet tall, which allow parents to see in and children to see out. Since it can be seen from all areas of the store by the parents, it is up to the parents to watch their own children. Inside are a few different toys that can be fun for kids while their parents shop. For parents that have young children, this may be a competitive advantage that you can advertise.

Designing your own child-play area can be very simple. First, find a small space in your store that can be used. For safety reasons, this area should not be near a door and should have some way of appearing confined. Play yard gates or inexpensive particle boards painted bright colors can be used to demarcate the area.

Once you find a space for your area, a few inexpensive toys are all that is needed. Building blocks, LEGO®, books, tea sets, and trains are inexpensive items that children love, require little maintenance, and can entertain

for hours. To save even more money, many of these items can be purchased at garage sales or flea markets. Some items should be avoided in your play area. Any toy that can be dangerous to children under three (e.g., jump ropes and toys with small parts), should not be included. Also, since your play area will need to be cleaned regularly, stay away from toys that are difficult to clean. Toys that can be cleaned with some diluted bleach will make your play area easier to maintain than toys that require special care. For instance, stuffed toys will get dirty very quickly and may make your play area seem dingy.

Of course, sometimes just having a few old toys from your own children at your store may be enough to entertain and amuse your customers' children. A local chiropractor brought three of his sons' old toys into his office and simply left them in the examination room. When they are not being used, they sit inconspicuously in a corner. However, when patients bring their children, the kids can be entertained quietly while their parents are examined.

Moneymaker: Children's toys can easily become a new revenue stream for your store. If you don't typically sell toys, there are still small, inexpensive items that can become perfect impulse purchases. Bouncing balls, neon necklaces, and inflatable toys can all be found online from many local and international vendors. Just make sure the products you choose have a high enough margin.

---

9. Reduce Shrinkage and Lost Dollars

When you are rearranging your products, consider the impact theft may be having on your store. Small items that can easily be pocketed may be stolen without your knowledge and large expensive items may be taken by bolder thieves. Therefore, review each of your products to determine how likely it is to be stolen. When rearranging, this risk should be taken into account.

Any expensive items should be stored in a locked case or locked down where they are displayed. For electronics such as laptops and cell phones, there are many "locks" available. While this will not increase your revenue, it will decrease the chance of loss due to theft. Therefore you may want to determine if the cost of purchasing a lock is less than the cost of the loss due to theft. In our retail business, a stolen laptop can cost more than $1,000 while the cost of a lock is less than $50. This type of cost/benefit analysis can help you determine if your business needs to invest in security.

Items that are too inexpensive to lock down but too small and costly to leave out should be located either near the register (where an employee can see them) or behind a glass case. Having small items near a register generally provides some security because shoplifters are more reluctant to steal when they might be closely observed. Once again, although this will not increase your gross sales, it should help decrease your shrinkage.

10. Keep Your Place of Business Organized and Clean

When your customers can tell that you are clean and organized it will improve their overall impression of your business. A store that is clean gives the impression that it values quality, while a messy store can make customers question its standards and the quality of the products. If a product or service is perceived to be of high quality, customers will instinctively believe it is more valuable and be willing to pay more. If it appears that the product is not a quality item, customers will be inclined to pay less. This isn't rocket science, but it's the type of thing that can slip over time if you're not careful. The following are a few basic things you can do to make sure your business leaves a good impression on your customers:

- Organize: When you are trying to reorganize your business, consider organizing areas to look less cluttered. For example, if you have a restaurant, you may want to ensure that the staff areas are organized and clean. The register area should be tidy. In a store, all stock should be labeled and neat. It's always easier to find things when they are stacked in an orderly fashion.

- Keep your bathrooms spotless: Bathrooms are considered by many to be a good indicator of general cleanliness. If bathrooms are clean, the assumption is that other parts of the business will also be clean. Therefore, it is very important to keep your bathrooms spotless. Even if the customers don't typically use the bathroom, occasionally they will. When they do, you want them to realize that cleanliness is important to your business.

- Maintain your front desk: Service areas can often become messy and unkempt. Keeping these in the front of the store can make even the neatest store appear disheveled. In one local shipping store, the owners carefully placed the shipping area in the back behind a four-foot desk. This allows the store to appear neat and clean when the customer first enters even if the shipping employees are boxing and packaging numerous items in the back.

- Clean back-office areas: Even areas your customers cannot commonly see should be clean and tidy. For instance, although most people don't see the kitchen in most restaurants, when the door opens it is easy to glance inside. How do you feel when you see a dirty, disorganized kitchen, with piles of used dishes and food sitting on counters? Even if your business doesn't serve food, your customers feel the same way about your back office. A disorganized, cluttered area may make customers believe that your customer service will be similarly muddled.

- Vacuum daily: Although your store may not get that dirty, vacuuming daily, or at least every other day, will ensure that the floors always look their best. This will make the store look larger (messes tend to make a room look smaller) and more inviting.

11. When to Implement Your New Design

Now that you have your design, the key is to implement it at the lowest cost possible. After you have determined what to do, you should choose a time to implement the change that will not have a large impact on your sales. Obviously if you feel you can handle the redecorating alone, completing it when the business is closed may make the most sense. However, since most businesses are open seven days a week, and most changes will require some employee assistance, this may not be possible. Instead, try to pick a date in the next month or so when your business sales will be typically slow. This may be the perfect time to rearrange your store.

Of course, just because your sales are slow doesn't mean you want to close to rearrange. Businesses today cannot afford to be closed for even one day. The cost of closing could multiply the cost of your remodel dramatically.

Therefore, even if you are planning to make a major renovation that moves all of your items, don't plan to close your business. Instead, take the time to plan your renovation in small sections. In other words, you should not plan to move all of your items at once. Review the new layout and the old layout and plan, on paper, how you can shift small individual sections. Each of these sections should be able to be completed by you and possibly one or two other employees in three or four hours. Breaking it down like this will allow you to manage the changes while keeping most of your store unaffected.

The renovation to our store involved approximately ten smaller moves that affected about 90 percent of the store. However, since this large change was completed in smaller chunks, customers were able to continue to purchase products and computer service was never interrupted.

By limiting your redesign to rearranging products and shelves and by completing these changes while your store is continuing to run, you can effectively implement a radical change at no cost to your business. This type of a redesign will improve your bottom line without increasing your expenses.

Lifesaver: One of the largest impact items — and the least expensive — is paint. Most small stores can be completely repainted in just a day or two and the cost will be less than $100. The impact is incredible. Scuff marks, paint chipping, and general wear and tear can make any store look dirty and unkempt. Repainting instantly makes a business look clean and inviting. Even if you can't do a large remodel, painting may make all the difference to your store's appearance.

15
ADAPT TO CHANGING MARKET CONDITIONS

In business, there are often economic storms that change the conditions of the market. Customers may cut back on disposable spending, new competitors may enter the market, and new products may suddenly appear. These radical changes can cause your business to suffer financially, if the company is not prepared to adapt. Fifty years ago a company may have been able to remain unchanged for decades, but in today's dynamic marketplace, this type of stagnation can often lead to failure. Instead, it is the businesses that can learn to reinvent themselves regularly that will be rewarded with growth and opportunity. Businesses that change to work within the new environment and become more competitive may find that these economic storms are actually welcome opportunities to grow and expand.

Of course, the most successful businesses do not need an economic problem to inspire the development of new business opportunities. Instead, these companies and their owners are constantly looking for new profitable products and services that can be offered to their customers. By constantly looking to grow, these businesses can survive any economy, and will grow in both good and bad markets.

One thing many business owners notice is that good ideas can often be recycled. Many of the suggestions in this book are used over and over by successful business owners whenever they find their market or customers have changed. Just because a decision was made that improved business two years ago doesn't mean that it will continue to be the right decision for the business's future. Being unafraid to change and adapt to new circumstances is the hallmark of a true entrepreneur.

For instance, we dramatically changed our store's layout just a few years ago. The goal at the time was to make more room for new products and computers. Once an economic slowdown hit a year or so later, we found that more of our customers were repairing old computers and less were buying new computers. We redesigned the store again, this time to make more room for service benches and repair shelves. Although it may seem like we were correcting a mistake, the original decision to change the layout of the store to show more new products was actually very valuable. Customers loved it and more computers sold than before.

Just because something worked in the past does not mean that it is necessary to be committed to that old decision. Each time a business faces a new challenge, the best way to approach it is by realizing that it is in fact a "new" challenge. If you remain committed to old decisions in the face of a new environment, you will never be able to adapt and grow with new opportunities.

1. Expand Your Service Offerings

Fortunately, there are many ways to expand your services without investing any money or taking any risks. Expanding the services that your business offers does not require high-end investments. There are many ways that small businesses can find more opportunities to sell to their customers, without investing any money in new offerings.

Unfortunately, not all businesses take advantage of opportunities to increase their revenue stream. For some reason, many businesses do not take the time to explore opportunities and instead simply reject customer requests. For example, one business we know is occasionally asked to ship its product out of state.

When customers ask for this service, they are told that the business doesn't provide shipping and the customers are instead instructed to buy the product and then use the shipping company right next door to ship the items. While this does satisfy some customers, it probably isn't the most profitable way to make the sale. In this example, offering a shipping option at a price that is profitable would be a convenience valuable to some customers. However, by not offering a shipping option the business risks losing a sale from loyal customers.

Unless you are certain that you cannot make a new opportunity profitable, rejections like the example are simply throwing money away. Companies make choices like this all the time. What is even worse about this scenario is that your customer still wants the product or service they thought you could provide. Most likely the customer will try another vendor. Once the customer goes to a competitor to get a service there is no guarantee he or she will return to your business. By ignoring the opportunity your business will not only lose a potential new sale and a new business opportunity, but it may have lost a customer as well! Think about what your company offers and what it doesn't. The following sections discuss some services you may want to consider offering.

1.1 At-home service

Determine how your products or services can be delivered directly to a customer's home. To figure out what you would charge for this service, consider these factors:

- The total cost of your time or the time of your employee. Make sure to include the fully loaded payroll costs for the time it takes to travel to the site, complete the work, and return to your store.

- Mileage reimbursement for the cost of the travel; include any tolls, or parking fees you may encounter.

- Add an additional 30 to 50 percent for your margin.

Remember the goal is to create profitable service. Even if the amount you are charging for this service seems high to you, new services should not be offered at a loss. Further, what may seem high to you may be reasonable for your customers.

1.2 Home delivery and shipping

For some businesses, "at-home service" isn't practical, but "at-home delivery" is. To ensure you charge enough for this service, get some standard rates from various shipping carriers and, of course, the post office. By comparing rates and finding a local drop point, you may find that shipping is easier and less expensive than you thought. To charge appropriately, make sure you include the following:

- Cost of shipping

- Cost of insurance (always add insurance, if possible)

- Cost of your packaging materials

- A handling fee to cover the time it will take you or your employees to ship the package

- An additional margin (i.e., 10 to 40 percent) on the handling fees

In this case, you will be able to make money on both the sale of the product as well as the shipping. If you are offering shipping for very high-end or highly profitable items, you may want to discount the additional shipping margin and charge the customer only the necessary shipping and handling costs.

 **Lifesaver:** Compare shipping companies before you choose a vendor. Many companies provide free packaging materials and sometimes free pickup. In some cases, it is even possible to create shipping labels online. Make sure to also check the post office because they can have very competitive pricing.

1.3 Online service

If your business already provides shipping and sells individual products at a retail store, why not have an online presence as well? While the costs of opening an online web business were high at one time, there are many options to expand to the Internet for a limited cost. For a few hundred dollars, many companies offer simple websites that include product displays, shopping carts, and credit card processing.

1.4 Product consulting

For some customers, having an individual to guide them in their decisions is very valuable. For a business, this can also be a very profitable service. In some cases, the company makes money through the purchases the customer will make because of this advice (as with a personal shopper who helps the customer choose clothing and accessories), but businesses can also make this a profitable service by offering it at an hourly rate. For small businesses, product consulting can simply take the form of ensuring that your experience and your employees' experience are shared with the customer.

1.5 Free product maintenance

After a customer purchases a product from your store, free product maintenance is a great way to ensure customer loyalty. It is generally a profitable service because it brings the customers back to your business regularly and helps them build trust in your business. An example of this type of service is a jewelry store in New York that encourages its customers to bring all their diamond jewelry back every six months so it can be cleaned and checked. Who wants to lose a valuable diamond because of a loose mounting? If any issue does arise, the customer will certainly hire that jeweler on the spot to make the necessary repair. This is a great service to provide the customers and while they are waiting for this service to be performed, they have the opportunity to view the new merchandise and possibly make additional purchases.

> # WARNING:
>
> Never lose money on a new service. When creating new pricing, include all the costs of doing business plus a comfortable margin. Never price a service by simply matching a competitor. Another company's costs to do business may not be the same as yours and you could lose money on any sales you make. Even if the service is offered at a higher price than other companies charge, your loyal customers may still purchase it as they appreciate the convenience of the new offering.

2. Expand by Selling to Local Businesses

One of the hardest parts about being a struggling business owner is waiting for customers to visit your store — so don't wait. Instead of sitting around, hoping your business will grow, kick-start the expansion by having you and your employees spend some time selling your service to other businesses. Although the cost of marketing to other businesses in person can be expensive — you will have to pay employees for their time and reimburse them for travel, tolls, and parking — it can be worth far more than the expenses. Finding new business customers can be especially lucrative since these customers are very likely to make regular, expected purchases.

With a little creativity, this type of marketing can work for just about any retail store. Everything from dry cleaners, to salons, to furniture stores can benefit by reaching out to the local businesses. For example, drycleaners can offer regular pickup and delivery services for employees; salons can provide on-site massages; and furniture stores can rent business furniture. Whatever your business, by reaching out to other companies, you will immediately receive feedback on your marketing as well as increase your sales. Also, the contacts you make can easily become referrals in the future. The following sections discuss how to target this market successfully.

2.1 Identify the company demographic you are targeting

Be specific about what type of business you want your sales staff to go after. This will help your employees know which type of businesses they should target with the new offers.

When we did this at our business, we looked for small businesses with three or more employees on staff with gross revenue of less than $5 million. These businesses were identified because they were the most likely to be large enough to need technical support, but small enough not to have an in-house resource already on staff. Make sure that your target business customers are easily identified and that your sales staff understands why they are being targeted.

2.2 Choose a repeatable offering

Choose something that the employees or business owners will be interested in purchasing repeatedly. This will necessarily vary by business. While our computer store offered regular maintenance contracts, a bakery may offer weekly "Monday Morning Muffin" delivery. Just make sure that the offering is something that the customer can use regularly — at least once a month.

2.3 Include an impulse purchase

As part of the sales campaign, try to include at least one or two items that a business can purchase immediately. Depending on your business, you could bring product samples with you or perhaps offer simple inspection services.

For example, in our computer store, we paired our sales staff with a technician and outfitted them with some additional RAM that could be installed right then and there in a client's computer to make it run faster. This allowed the business customer to make a low-cost purchase that immediately had a positive impact on his or her business.

2.4 Leave a flyer or advertisement with the potential business customer

After you leave, you want to ensure that the business will remember your company. Arm your sales staff with some flyers or ads about your business. For a restaurant, this may mean leaving your menu; for a service-consulting business, this may mean a folder with detailed information about your business history and services. Whatever you do, ensure that your materials are professional and highlight the repeatable offering you were there to sell.

Moneymaker: Try to visit businesses during their least busy times. For most companies, the best time will generally be early in the morning, when the owner and the employees have arrived but before customers have started calling. Cold calls or visits received during busy times will not receive much attention — if any. However, sales calls made when business is slow will be given more time and will be more profitable.

3. Finding Profitable Partnerships

As a business owner, you will probably have the chance to meet more business owners than you ever did before. Therefore, you will also find new opportunities to partner with other businesses that you may have never considered. The key is to be able to offer another business owner ways to partner that are profitable for both of your businesses. To do this you may have to think outside of your normal market or industry.

This can be done in a number of simple ways. One way is to try to offer discounts on low-cost services to new customers. Of course, the customers targeted by your current marketing, advertising, and referrals are not the type of customers you want to target with this low offer. You want individuals that maybe would not otherwise know about your products or services. That is where a partnership with another local business can come in handy. By targeting customers that are normally out of your reach, you can open your business to entirely new markets.

A local paintball company has this idea perfected. Their business makes money in three different ways: renting the paintball equipment, selling paintballs, and selling food and drinks while the customer is playing. Obviously, in order to sell food and paintballs, the company must lay out the initial cost for the products. However, with equipment rental, the company has already purchased the equipment. If it is not used, for even one day, the company is out the opportunity cost of the sale. Therefore, to the paintball company, providing the rental equipment to a new customer for a very low introductory rate is a great way to get another person hooked on paintball while also selling ancillary products (e.g., paintballs and refreshments).

Their sales team goes from business to business, offering day rentals of all the equipment for paintball at a low-cash price. However, they also take it one step further. Aside from taking the opportunity to sell their product, they also look for opportunities to partner with other business owners. Their goal is to find complementary companies whose patrons might become customers of the paintball company. To these businesses, they offer a partnership. When a customer purchases a big-ticket item from a partner business, the paintball company throws in two tickets for full rental equipment for a day. The partnership works well because the paintball company finds a new customer without having to invest any hard dollars in advertising or salespeople, and the partner company can advertise the tickets to help close the sale. By creating synergies like these, both companies have the opportunity to increase revenue and propel their growth.

If you have a retail store, you may also want to increase your revenues by selling additional products and services from local reputable vendors. To do this, you simply find another business in the area that will allow you to sell product on its behalf for a flat commission.

There are many businesses that will be willing to do this. Just make sure that you partner with products that are in your line of business but not competing with it.

Over the years, our computer store has partnered with various companies that have related products. As a reseller, we did not have to invest in purchasing the new product or commit to any up-front cost, yet we receive a commission on each sale we make. Thus, we can expand our product offering in a noncompetitive area and without increasing our costs.

Another type of partnership some businesses create is an outsourcing relationship. In this case, the order is purchased through your business and you can outsource the work to another vendor either with or without the customer's knowledge. Whatever type of partnership you arrange, vet the partner business carefully before you commit to a relationship like this. Once you choose to partner with any other company, their workmanship will reflect positively or negatively on your business. For example, let's say you own a jewelry store and you have a jeweler on site, but he or she is unfamiliar with watch repair, so you partner with a watchmaker. If you don't take the time to check the watchmaker's workmanship or quality, and he or she turns out to have poor skills, your business's reputation could be damaged.

4. Taking Advantage of Free Ideas to Continue to Grow

At some point, you will realize that you have implemented all of the best ideas that you and your employees have to increase your sales. Don't worry, there is still one other group that will always be able to provide ideas and inspiration for new revenue sources: your customers.

When customers ask you for new services they are actually providing you with ideas for new ways to generate revenue as well as the opportunity to test your pricing structure. The next time a customer inquires about a service you don't provide or a product you don't carry, instead of dismissing it, agree and say that you just have to check the costs. At that point, do some fast math. Take a moment to include all of the costs you will incur, both through employee time and through the products. Then add in your normal margin for services and see what the customer says. If he or she agrees, you have just created a profitable new service. If not, you have still given the person an option and showed that you would work with your customers to meet their needs. Either way, the business wins.

5. Markets and Customers Change — So Should You!

The day your business started is the day your market began to change. Today's economy is dynamic. New products are constantly brought to market, customer expectations change, and new competitors emerge and disappear. Therefore, it is up to you to make your business thrive under these ever-changing circumstances. What worked in the past may not work in the future.

One great example of a changing market is what happened to the buggy whip companies when the car started being mass-produced by Ford. The new mode of transportation was such an improvement over the old-fashioned carriage and buggy that companies that specialized in this area couldn't compete. They tried to improve the carriages and even came out with a better buggy whip, but to no avail. The carriage could not compete against the car. Soon after, most of the carriage and buggy whip companies were out of business.

The story about the buggy whip companies has been repeated many times as a lesson that you can't always compete against a better product. However, that may not be the right lesson to take from this example. What is more fascinating is not the discovery that companies failed to compete in a new market — after all, 99 percent of all businesses fail in the first ten years. Failing is not remarkable. What is more remarkable is that some of the buggy whip companies did *not* go out of business. Some survived and are still around today. These companies knew how to adapt, change, and even thrive.

Today, if you search for "buggy whips" on the Internet, you will find many companies that specialize in this service including Jedediah's Buggy Whip in Nebraska. Jedediah's boasts that they have been "repairing buggy whips and horse tack by hand since 1853!" You can imagine that in the 1930s when other buggy whip companies were closing their doors, this company was redefining themselves to survive. Today, Jedediah's Buggy Whip receives repair requests from all over the world. Their customers vary from individuals who still enjoy this traditional mode of transportation to historical societies that need replicas made or antiques repaired.[1]

Therefore, the lesson from the buggy whips is that a company can survive just about any market change, any competition, and any challenge as long as they are willing to adjust to the new market conditions. While markets may change, it is companies that have this type of adaptability that will be profitable and able to continue to grow.

---

[1] Jedediah's Buggy Whip, "Welcome" and "Overview," http://jedediahsbuggywhip.com (May 2009).

16
COMPETE EFFECTIVELY WITH BIG BUSINESSES

Gone are the days when a small-business owner had nothing more than local competition. Today, big-box stores have sprung up in almost every industry and field. The local hardware store now competes with giants such as The Home Depot and Lowe's. The neighborhood butcher has competition from every nearby chain supermarket. For that matter, just about every small business finds itself competing in some way with the local Wal-Mart.

While some business owners see the installation of a nearby large competitor as something to fear, other companies have learned to embrace these competitors and thrive, even in their shadow. These entrepreneurs have found that large companies may actually be good for their business.

1. Don't Compete on Their Terms

One of the biggest mistakes a small business can make is to try to compete head-to-head with a large box store on the large store's platform. For instance, Wal-Mart is known as a low-price leader. If your business had been the local low-price seller for a particular type of product, such as paint, you may find that having a Wal-Mart in your area is now impacting your sales. As an owner, you now have a choice — you can continue to attempt to compete on the low-cost platform or you can adapt. However, if you attempt to go head to head with Wal-Mart on price, odds are not good that you will win. Typically, these large chain companies can provide a larger variety of products (they have a larger store size) at a lower cost (they are purchasing in larger volume) than your small business can ever hope to sell. Since many of these box chains strive to be the low-cost provider, if you find you are now competing with one of these businesses, it is important to define your business in a new way that is not in direct competition with the advertising of the national brand. No business, no matter how large, can ever be all things to all people. Therefore, it is important to identify how your business can effectively market itself against the larger competitor without competing directly.

There are not many businesses that have been able to compete effectively with Wal-Mart on price. However, there are many businesses that have found that having large stores such as Wal-Mart in their area has actually improved their sales! Since these large companies cannot provide specialized products and services, many of their sales associates will refer customers to local businesses that can help. As a result, some small businesses will grow significantly from these referrals. Although our computer store is relatively small, we have received referrals from many large chains including some that offer computer repairs and service. The reason is because we provide unique services that large chains can't offer.

Moneymaker: Even though most companies cannot afford the large advertising budget of a national chain, it is still possible to generate the same amount of buzz for next to nothing. Anything from viral YouTube videos to unusual newspaper ads can draw attention and increase customers. Years ago, this was referred as a publicity stunt; today it is called Guerilla Marketing. Either way it can be a great way to bring in new revenue.

2. Stand out in a Crowd

When you are competing against a large company or even a bunch of small companies, it helps to be able to stand apart from the rest. This does not mean that you have to change your processes, your products, or your service. If the fundamentals that support your business are sound, they should remain to provide consistency for your customers. In this case, standing out may be as simple as making small changes in unique ways.

Take the McDonald's at 160 Broadway in New York City. They are known worldwide, although they remain a traditional, loyal McDonald's.

McDonald's has one of the best processes in place for running a franchise. They are known for their ability to train owners and employees to ensure consistent service at each franchise location. No one who owns or operates a McDonald's franchise would want to deviate from this successful model.

Yet this one location in New York City has found a way to stand out as a unique, special restaurant. Unlike any other McDonald's, this one prides itself on providing high class and luxury — it boasts marble tables, fresh flowers, and even a musician playing a baby grand piano upstairs.[1] The differences from a normal McDonald's are striking and impressive to the average customer. At the same time the fundamentals of the business are still the same. The burgers, fries, and other menu items are still served in the same way using the same process. Yet, customers visit this restaurant for the experience as well as the food.

To find a way for your business to stand out, look for something that will draw attention while improving the general customer

---

[1] Lower Manhattan Construction Command Center, "For 39 Cents More, Super-Size the Baby Grand," http://www.lowermanhattan. info/news/for_39_cents_more_86728.aspx (September 19, 2002).

experience. Just be sure that whatever you offer is cost-effective, related to your brand, and will be appreciated by your customers, since you will be counting on your customers to spread the word about your unusual offerings.

Moneymaker: If you want customers to recognize your brand, try to find an advertising gimmick. Choosing a unique icon for your business is a great way to increase your visibility and stand out. Don't worry if it is silly or unusual — the more attention it generates, the more sales you will get. Once you find your unique icon, make sure to trademark it.

3. Personalize Your Presentation

Not everyone likes the idea of buying products from a large impersonal company. Many people like the service and personalization that comes from working with a smaller, local business, even if they have to pay a little bit more. Since your business is smaller, make sure that your employees focus on the following benefits for your customers:

- Some customers like to work with smaller businesses so that they can have the opportunity to deal directly with the owner. Make sure your employees know you are available to any customer that wants to deal directly with you.

- Personalize customer service, call customers by name, and if you have regular customers, make sure that you, the owner, know them by name.

- Send thank-you notes to your customers, directly from the employee who dealt with that customer. This old-fashioned tradition is a great personal touch.

- Offer your customers something to drink while they shop; for example, coffee, tea, or water are low-cost beverages that appeal to most customers.

- Work within your local community. If your business donates money or products, contributing to local charities is a great way to help your community and get some publicity.

Moneymaker: Another way to make people aware of your business is to create advertising cards. These small business-sized cards can contain a discount or offer for new customers. Once you have them, give them out freely. When you are in a restaurant, leave one with your tip; when you are in a parking lot, leave one on the car next to you. For a small investment, you will increase your advertising and your customer list.

4. Find Your Unique and Uncommon Products

Many large companies that are selling on price alone usually only have one or two low-cost brands. In general, large retailers will try to have the most popular products in their stores to ensure that the most customers are served. In this case, the easiest way to compete is to become known as the specialty retailer. For example, there is a local store in our area that specializes in fixing computers, but not all computers — this company's specialization is laptops. While this may not sound like much, fixing laptops is actually a specialized skill set. The computers are built differently from desktop computers, requiring different tools to open and different parts to repair. As a result, many other businesses, such as our own computer store, send customers over to this specialized company!

In order to find your unique and uncommon products, ask yourself the following questions:

- Do you have any unique items in your inventory?

- Are there any services that your company offers that most large chains do not?

- Are there any products that you carry that are local and, therefore, not carried by large warehouse stores?

- Do you have more specialized products than a large vendor would want to carry?

Moneymaker: Check your business hours against other businesses. Also check the time other businesses in your immediate complex are open. If your hours are very different from the other businesses in the market and in your area, you may be missing sales! Increasing your hours to match your customers' expectations may be a simple way of raising new revenue.

5. Sell Your Company's Industry Knowledge

When you think of telemarketing, you probably think of large marketing companies that dial your home during dinner and try to sell you the latest and greatest product or service. However, telemarketing is used in a variety of ways to advertise many different services.

We know one business that has been around for decades in the telemarketing industry and because of the owner's specialized knowledge

has no other competitors in that niche. This company is a telemarketing firm that specializes in a very specific area. The company exclusively makes calls for Christian church planters. Since the owner has decades of experience in this field, the company not only provides the telemarketing, but the owner also gives specialized guidance and coaching that could not be found with any other provider. As a result, this business has grown and continues to thrive without any real competition from any other vendor!

In order to sell your company's industry knowledge, ask yourself the following questions:

- Do you have any unique knowledge or experience that cannot be replicated by others in the industry?

- Do your employees have more knowledge than the typical employee at your larger competitor?

- Do you offer additional, complimentary training, customization, or advice when your customer buys your products?

6. Be Prepared for Direct Competition

In almost any business, at some point, you will find your customers asking how your products compare to those at another vendor. Be prepared to answer these questions. If your competitors send out regular flyers, you should try to obtain these weekly so that you know what the local vendors are selling and so you will not be surprised when your customers bring them in. Also, this will help you prepare your products' selling points.

Another area you should be prepared to discuss is your business's differences from other vendors in the area. Bring up your experience in the industry, the personalized customer service, customized products, and whatever distinguishes your business. These items will help you stand apart from large box stores.

Our store, Arizona Computer Outlets, prides itself on helping customers purchase only what they need. Everything from the "Free, no obligation, 15-minute computer diagnostic," to the variety of computers in the store (e.g., everything from low-end used machines to high-end gaming computers), lets customers know that the business does not try to push the same solution or same products on each customer. When customers come in with an ad from a competitor, we help them understand what they need, not what some salesperson working on commission wants them to have.

7. Be Positive If You Want to Win Customers

One mistake some employees and sometimes business owners make is to focus too much discussion on the competition and not enough on your products or services. Whenever you discuss your competition with your customers, make sure that you constantly emphasize the positive benefits of your product and try not to focus on the negative aspects of the competitor — or the competitor at all. Customers often have strong opinions about products and by trying to malign a competing product you may actually turn off or offend a customer. By focusing on the benefits of your product or service, you are educating the customers on your brand and making their shopping a positive experience.

17
TAKE ADVANTAGE OF BARTER OPPORTUNITIES

When a ship captain left port, he typically planned to take goods to the next destination so he could trade for other items once he arrived. Since he was traveling to foreign lands, and no currency was available that could be transferred from country to country, trade was the only way to make his trip pay off. Today, with the advent of modern currencies and conversion rates, business owners often forget that all business originally began as trade. However, a business that is familiar with bartering can quickly expand its customer list, grow its revenue, and decrease its cost of doing business.

1. What Is Barter?

Today, cash is so ubiquitous that it is hard to imagine life without it. Even when we pay by credit card or check, we are using the cash value to measure an item's value. However, it wasn't too long ago that barter was the most common method of trading goods and services. In small towns around the world, the individual "business owners" that ran the local bakeries, smiths, and farmers commonly traded goods and services with each other. The difficulty of trade was that individuals had to decide what a particular good or service was worth. For example, we know one business owner that owned and ran a business about 30 years ago in rural California. He was in the business of creating artificial teeth for his customers. In his area, barter was still alive and well. His customers frequently offered payment in terms of goods instead of dollars. As a matter of fact, he once accepted a Holstein cow as payment for a set of teeth!

Of course, barter has come a long way over the years and today barter can take many forms. You can still choose to trade goods for goods (e.g., deciding that one set of artificial teeth is worth one cow). Or you can choose to get involved in a formal barter program that manages the trades for you and even handles tax reporting.

However you choose to do it, barter allows you to conduct normal, everyday business without spending or receiving any cash. In many ways, we barter every day. For example, your sister asks you to watch her kids one Saturday night and then she returns the favor the next weekend. In our normal day-to-day lives, trading favors is very common. In business it can be just as valuable, even if it is less commonly used. It can save you money, bring in new customers, and help grow your business revenue. For instance, we had a plumbing issue the same day a plumber brought his computer in to be repaired. The solution was obvious; we fixed his computer while he fixed our plumbing problem. No dollars changed hands. Plus, since neither of us paid with a credit card we each saved the 2 to 5 percent fee the credit card company would have taken from the transaction. In this case, barter allowed us both to benefit. We were able to repair the plumbing issue without spending any cash, he was able to get his computer fixed without spending any cash and we both had our repairs completed the same day. The situation was a win-win for both of our businesses!

WARNING:

Always treat barter transactions just like regular transactions in your business. Follow the normal process with customers, complete all appropriate paperwork and make sure to provide an itemized bill. Barter transactions need to comply with any legal or tax obligations. Check with your accountant or lawyer if you aren't sure how to handle trades.

2. Why Barter?

The more product and services a business sells the better. Barter is just another way of expanding your sales to another group of potential buyers. Selling your products for cash is no different from bartering your products for other goods and services. The only significant difference is that many businesses and customers are more likely to buy when they know they can barter than they are when they have to pay cash. Why? In general, the world is a very cash-oriented place. Having cash in your pocket provides a feeling of safety, security, and opportunity. Once you spend cash, you lose the opportunity to spend it somewhere else. With barter, the opposite is true. Most people feel that they and their business have extra capacity that is not being used. When you offer people the opportunity to trade, they feel they can absorb the work without increasing their costs. To them, the cost of the trade is now virtually free. This is especially true if your customers have a limited cash supply — you may find that they are willing to trade just to be able to save that cash.

Let's take the example from section **1.** about the plumber who came into our store to have his computer fixed. He wasn't excited about spending his hard earned cash to do it. When we presented him with the option of repairing our plumbing, he now had a different decision. He already spent the time to get to our store to bring in his computer, so there was no cost to travel. Further, he had all the experience and training necessary to analyze and solve our issue, so he didn't have to call in anyone and pay the employee for his or her time. Therefore, instead of waiting for the next couple of hours for his computer to be repaired, he had the option of completing some simple plumbing repairs and getting his machine fixed for close to nothing! If this wasn't enough, he was able to get other benefits as well. Before he brought his computer to the store, we hadn't even heard of him. Therefore, we would not have called him for the repair. Taking the trade gave him the opportunity to get another customer and expand his business. Not a bad day's work for someone who thought he would be wasting the day getting a computer fixed!

What are the real benefits of barter for businesses? There are significant benefits for both the seller and the buyer as discussed in the following sections.

2.1 Seller benefits of barter

The seller can benefit from bartering by getting increased sales, expanding the customer base, reducing costs on sales, and resolving disputes more easily.

2.1a Increased sales

Many people feel more comfortable purchasing items on barter than they would if they used cash. You may find that customers that had previously turned down a purchase will be more amiable if they discover they can barter for it instead. Because many of these individuals are trading service for service, they are simply trading their time for something that they want. To many, this trade time is easier than parting with cash.

2.1b Expanded customer base

There are some businesses that really love to barter and have basically found that they will only barter for certain goods and services. Therefore, by opening your business up to barter, you will be expanding your customer base to an entirely new market.

2.1c Reduced costs on every sale

When you barter, you typically have lower costs on each transaction. For instance, when you make a typical $100 sale, you have to pay between 2 to 5 percent in fees to the credit card company if the person pays by credit card. This can take up to $5 off the profitability of the sale. Since you are trading outright with the other business, there is no need to process a credit card transaction.

2.1d Easier resolution of disputes

When you have a dissatisfied customer who pays by credit card, the customer can simply dispute the charges and the seller can lose the entire payment. Similarly, when a customer pays by check, the buyer can just stop payment on the check. When a customer pays by barter, the transaction is more like a cash transaction in that the buyer cannot surprise the seller by taking back his or her money. Therefore, if there is an issue, it is typically resolved between the two parties without dragging in banks and credit card companies.

Moneymaker: When you barter do not offer discounts, incentives, or other sales to the barter customer. In general, barter is completed at market price on both sides. The only time you may want to discount your products or services is when the totals are close on both sides. If you find that one bill is $225, and the other is $240, you may just want to call it even to simplify the transaction.

2.2 Buyer benefits of barter

The buyer benefits by getting increased purchasing power, more leverage, and greater speed and flexibility with transactions.

2.2a Increased purchasing power

When a buyer has to pay with cash, or even a credit card, he or she has to pay it off with other sales. Unfortunately, you can't be sure when you are making these sales and when you will be able to profit enough to pay the bill. With barter, you already know how you will pay the bill — the sale you make to the customer!

2.2b More leverage

When you are a onetime customer of a business, you may find that you just get lumped in with other customers. When you work a barter deal, you typically have more leverage to ensure your sale is completed right. Since you are bartering you will typically work with the other business owner, so you get the best, personalized service! Plus, since you are completing service for him or her, you can be sure he or she wants to make sure you do your best as well.

2.2c Greater speed and flexibility

Very often, when you barter, you try to complete both sides of the trade at the same time. Therefore, you may find that your transactions are completed faster than normal. Since both businesses have something the other wants, chances are that both owners are willing to "fit in the work" to ensure both projects are completed quickly. You typically will not get this type of service when you are just another customer.

 **Lifesaver:** In general, make it your policy to complete both sides of a trade close to the same time. When you enter into a barter trade, like any transaction, there is an element of risk. Will the buyer actually pay as promised? Having both sides of the transaction completed around the same time ensures both parties that the transaction will go smoothly.

3. Taxes and Barter

Before you start bartering you have to understand a few legal rules. First of all, the Internal Revenue Service (IRS) and the Canada Revenue Agency's (CRA) positions on bartering are that if you trade goods or services, you are legally obligated to report the income. Therefore, barter does not exclude your legal obligations to pay taxes on the services or goods that you barter. For instance, if you barter $50 in merchandise and $50 in service, you are legally obligated to report the sale. For the IRS and CRA, you must pay appropriate taxes on the total $100 sale.

For your local government obligations, you may be required to collect sales tax if sales tax is typically collected on the merchandise you sold. For instance, in Arizona, the sale of a computer is taxable and sales tax would need to be collected and reported. Services are not taxable but are reportable.

It is recommended that you keep track of your barter transactions just as you would any other business transaction. For us, we enter each transaction into our books, print our customers a receipt, and simply attribute the "payment" to barter rather than a credit card, cash, or check transaction. We can then properly report to the IRS and our state and local government. To determine what is the best way for your business to track these transactions check with your personal accountant or bookkeeper.

4. Finding Businesses That Will Barter

Although it may seem difficult to find businesses that barter, it has been our experience that most business owners will consider barter. Therefore the easiest way to find someone to barter with is to consider what services or merchandise you are looking to purchase.

Then, you just need to decide whom you want to approach. There are benefits to approaching existing customers and offering a trade, but even more benefits of trying to find new customers to trade with. For instance, let's say you are looking for accounting services. First, determine what you have that is most flexible for trade. For instance, a Chinese restaurant nearby once offered us a few hundred dollars in meals to repair their computers — they were a great restaurant, so it wound up being a great barter deal!

Once you have identified your tradeable product or service, the next step is finding the business with which you want to trade. Ideally, smaller, owner-run businesses will be much more agreeable to barter than larger establishments. Since most businesses are in relatively commercial areas, you should be able to find another small company in your area that specializes in the service you need. Call the company and ask to speak directly to the owner. Explain your proposition, what you offer and what you would like in return. You may be surprised how many people will agree to the terms just to make a new sale and gain a new customer.

Moneymaker: Don't be afraid to add a cash component to a barter sale. For instance, if what you want to purchase comes to $200, while what the other business owner wants to purchase totals $350, do not feel pressured to call it an even trade. Instead, offer to add a cash component to the sale and ask the person to pay the difference of $150.

Another way to find new customers is through the Internet. Trading sites such as Craigslist.org allow you to put your goods and services online and even specify what you would like to exchange. While these ads are not as targeted, you can get some great responses. Further, reading through these ads will give you an idea of which business owners in your area are looking to barter. You may find more opportunities than you originally anticipated.

Bartering may also allow you to increase your current sales. For instance, some business owners we have spoken with have said that they would buy products or services once they get more cash. If you want to purchase something from these businesses, you may be able to convince them to complete the sale now with your company by offering to take a part of the sale in barter.

4.1 Bartering within a barter group

One of the easiest and fastest ways to jump into barter is to join a barter group. When you choose to join a barter group, you can join a larger network of individuals who are already interested in trading goods and services. The barter service we joined, Premier Barter, was able to get us in touch with many legitimate businesses in our area that had experience and standing in the barter community. They have an online site that acts as a trading forum. Unlike business-to-business barter, once you are part of a good barter group it is no longer necessary to trade services directly with an individual business. Instead, the items are posted "for sale" the same way they are in any listing. Information is listed about the business, the services, and a "dollar" cost of the service. Businesses in the barter program can then choose to "purchase" services at the agreed upon amount. However, unlike business-to-business barter, using a network barter service allows you to barter for "barter dollars" (which are similar to regular dollars in terms of value).

The way it works is simple. You post your merchandise and services online. Then, whenever another member of the barter group wants to purchase a product or service, they search through these ads until they find a company and product that is appealing. At this point, you can sell your service to any company in the barter network and receive "barter dollars" that you can spend at any business in the barter network. For example, let's say that we want to buy accounting for the year and we have computer repairs to offer. We sell computer repair services to three or four companies at the local going rate. The transaction is completed just like any other customer sale. The customer brings the computer to our store and goes through the normal process. When the customer is checked out we give them a normal receipt but we also add the transaction into the barter system. After a few new sales, let's say our business has accumulated about $500 in barter dollars in our barter account; at this point, we can spend those barter dollars with any vendor, including the accounting company we would like to work with. If the accounting company only charges $450 to complete the taxes, then we keep the extra $50 in our barter account for the next trade. In this way, barter dollars works just like regular dollars.

Joining a barter group typically costs a nominal fee. In addition, these networks will charge a small fee for each transaction to cover the costs of processing the trade, managing the service, and handling the tax filings (network barter groups typically file with the IRS and CRA and provide you a copy of the filing). This fee, which is dramatically lower than most other advertising fees, is worthwhile as it will open your business to an entire network of potential customers. Some benefits of a joining a barter group include:

- Businesses included in the network already understand and want to participate in barter.

- Businesses that are unethical or illegitimate will typically be screened out by a good barter group (they probably won't want to pay the fee).

- Barter groups handle filing with the IRS and CRA and provide you with detailed documentation on your trades.

- You can trade barter dollars instead of goods and services. This means that you no longer have to trade directly with just one company at a time. You can sell services and products to any business in the group and spend your barter dollars with any business in the group; you no longer have to do a business-to-business trade.

- You have a new group of customers immediately interested in your advertising. Typically, the businesses in your barter group won't all be businesses you have been working with in the past. As a result, you have a new source of customers and clients for the one-time cost of joining the network.

Another nice thing about being part of a barter group is that you now have the ability to help expand your business and your barter network. For instance, if you are approached by a company you don't want to trade with but one that wants to trade with you, you can now invite them to join the barter network. When they join, you can complete your part of the transaction, increasing your barter dollars and you will then be able to spend that money any way you see fit!

While we participated in barter at first by doing individual trades, it can be time consuming to find individuals to trade with. Joining a barter group expanded sales, and was able to reduce our fixed costs by allowing us to obtain bartered business services. Within the first few months we received many hits and quickly built up barter dollars that we were able to start spending. In fact, many of the businesses we work with agree that since they joined Premier Barter their business has had thousands of dollars in new sales. One business owner in construction found that since he joined the group he had accumulated more than $10,000 in barter dollars.

> **WARNING:**
>
> Do not allow your employees the authority to enter into barter transactions without your approval. Since barter transactions are typically very flexible, if an employee is not familiar with the trade process, it is possible for an employee to commit your business to a trade that is not in the best interest of your business.

5. Paying Your Expenses through Barter

If you take the time to get involved with barter and join a barter group, you may find that you have suddenly accumulated a significant number of new customers and new barter dollars. The next step is determining how you can now use these dollars to reduce your expenses. Because barter dollars may seem easy to make, it's tempting to squander them all on fun trips and merchandise. While it is usually easy to trade for just about anything, the key is to first get this new revenue stream to pay for purchases you need to make anyway. Thus, the barter dollars that your business is earning is actually paying your bills!

5.1 Paying your bills through barter

When you start to actively barter, you will find that many service-oriented businesses are willing to barter. Therefore, there is a great opportunity to reduce your business's monthly cash bills by using barter. Chances are there are services you already purchase that you can transfer over. Some candidates for switching from your current vendor to a barter company include:

- Accounting (e.g., yearly taxes, regular payroll)
- Bookkeeping (e.g., monthly management and reporting)
- Legal services (e.g., business entity creation, filing articles)
- Pest control (e.g., onsite spraying)
- Technical support (e.g., computer services, repair, regular maintenance)

When our business went through this exercise, we took a rigid stance and transferred any service to a barter vendor even if we liked the original provider. While this may sound difficult to do at first, the payoff was worthwhile; our business saved thousands of dollars in cash each year.

5.2 Paying yourself through barter

As a business owner, you typically pay yourself some sort of salary or profit sharing. Therefore, you can also use barter to chase goods and services for your own personal use. In this case, you have to make sure that you are handling the purchases you make as money drawn from the business and as always, should check with your bookkeeper or accountant to make sure you are following all the appropriate rules for your business. However, once you determine how you can pay yourself through barter, you may find a wealth of services that you can barter such as the following:

- Gardening (e.g., lawn care, tree maintenance)

- Pool service (e.g., regular maintenance, repairs)

- Personal accounting, bookkeeping, or legal services

- Merchandise — this can vary wildly from furniture to jewelry to children's toys

- Vacations (e.g., trips that can include hotel accommodations)

- Restaurant bills

5.3 Paying your employees through barter

Obviously, barter will not allow you to pay any cash bill with barter dollars; however, this doesn't mean that you can't reduce your employee expenses with barter. For instance, there are times when you may have an employee complete overtime to perform a particular task. If that task can be outsourced, chances are you can barter it. Some ways to reduce employee expenses through barter include:

- Outsource employee tasks to reduce head count: Look at your employee tasks and determine if any can be given to another vendor. For example, if you have a part-time bookkeeper, why not outsource the task to a bookkeeping firm for barter? You will reduce your employee overhead and be able to spend your barter dollars.

- Employee bonuses: With the range of items offered on barter, you can change employee bonuses from cash to simple gifts such as restaurant gift certificates or vacations.

- Company team building: Instead of paying for off-site team building activities, take your employees to a vendor in your barter network.

- Employee salaries: Occasionally, your business will have a product or service that your employees want to purchase. Rather than going through an official sale, you can also choose to barter with your employees to make the trade.

Just remember to contact your accountant to ensure that all bartering you do with your employees is consistent with local laws. In some cases the employee benefit may need to be included in the employees' payroll as it may be considered a taxable benefit.

6. You Can Barter for Anything

Now that you are looking to barter, the limit of what you can barter is only based on which businesses you barter with, so what you can barter for is virtually unlimited. While joining a barter group will give you a good start into barter, if you want something done or if you want to make a purchase and don't have the cash, there is no reason you can't find another owner to barter with. Just make sure you always check with your accountant or bookkeeper to ensure that you are adhering to all accounting regulations.

18
PROTECT YOUR BUSINESS FROM THEFT AND FRAUD

Instead of working to build successful companies of their own, thieves and fraudsters spend their lives trying to find ways to defraud legitimate businesses. The same attention you pay to your business, you can bet they spend learning their own trade. Unfortunately, this means that you can't avoid these unethical individuals, so instead you have to implement business rules designed to protect your business.

While it is often tempting to bend the rules a bit to be more flexible for your customers, there are many business owners who, after having been burned themselves, will tell you to never make exceptions once you implement your rules. Unfortunately, we know of a store owner who lost his business due to fraud. A customer called with a very large order. The store typically had gross receipts of only $10,000 to $20,000 per month; however, this order was for $50,000! In one order, the store owner realized he could make the same amount as he would normally make in two and a half months. Needless to say he jumped at the opportunity, eager to make the deal work. The store owner purchased the product up-front and asked the customer for only a small down payment to keep the customer happy. The store owner then shipped the product to the customer and took a credit card as payment. Unfortunately the deal was a scam. Before it was over, the store lost the entire shipment of product and was left with bills it could not afford to pay. The business had to declare bankruptcy to get out of the debt.

1. The Risks of Accepting Checks

Passing fraudulent checks is probably one of the more common scams. As a result, many business owners make it a policy not to accept checks from their customers. Occasionally, our business will accept checks from businesses that we work with regularly, but, as a rule, the potential for check fraud is too significant to accept checks. Unfortunately, most business owners will try to accept checks at some point in the course of business, and tend to run into the following cons.

The most obvious con is the individual that writes a bad check. For example, Dave walks into your store, wants to make a purchase but he has forgotten his wallet. He doesn't have the cash, and instead offers a check. You accept the check and when your bank tries to process it you discover that Dave does not have the money to pay. Not only are you out the cost of the product you sold, but your bank will typically charge you an insufficient funds fee that can cost up to $25.

After the experience with Dave, you learn not to accept checks without sufficient funds in the account. At the next check sale, you calls the bank directly to verify that Beth's account has enough funds to cover her check. The bank confirms that Beth has the money to pay the bill. The check is accepted and at the end of the day the owner runs over to the bank to deposit the new check. Two days later, another charge shows up on your bill for insufficient funds. Although Beth had the money in her account the day the business received the check, by the time the check cleared the bank, the customer's funds were gone and the check bounced.

Now it is technically possible to get the money back. Theoretically, you can take the customer to court — small claims court if the amount is low enough — and make a claim against the person. You can take the issue to a collection agency and if the agency can collect any money, it will take a percentage of the collected money. Unfortunately, the amount of time you will invest in this process is significant and the odds of getting your money back are low. As a result, many small-business owners find that the risk of accepting a check does not exceed the profit that can be made on a sale. For example, if you want to sell a product for $100 and the cost of the product is $60, you have invested $60 of your own money in the sale. If the check bounces, you will have lost your $60 plus the bounced check fee of $20 for a total loss of $80. However, if the check is good, then you will make $40. This means that for every bad check you receive you have to make two more sales to cover what you lost! Because of this, many business owners decide that it is easier and less expensive to avoid dealing with the risk of checks.

There are a handful of times when you will probably want to accept checks. For instance, if your business involves selling services or renting products with a very low investment, you may want to consider accepting checks. For example, if you run a bowling alley, you may want to consider accepting checks for rentals and games during off-peak hours. In this case, you have already spent money to open the business, so even if all of the checks don't clear, the ones that will may be enough to offset the bounced check fees and add some profit to your business. Another situation in which you might accept checks is if you regularly sell to another business. Even if the check is bad, the laws around debt recovery make it easier to recover money from a business than it is from an individual.

If you must accept checks, make sure to follow these simple guidelines that will help you create a formal check policy for your business:

- Require photo identification (ID), such as a driver's license and check that the name, address, and signature on the check match the name, address, and signature on the ID.

- Require that the check be written and signed in front of the seller.

- Require that the check be drawn from a local back (which means the check will cash faster).

- Do not allow a check to be written for more than the purchase prices; in other words, never give cash back on a check.

- Do not allow post-dated checks. This means that the customer should not try to get you to cash the check later in the week or month.

- Cash checks quickly. Most banks won't cash checks that are more than three to six months old.

- Verify that the amount written in words matches the amount written in numbers. Some banks won't cash checks that don't match at all, while others will use the words over the numbers.

- Do not accept checks that have any indication of being altered. There are many counterfeit scams that occur, so if you are unsure, it is better to lose the sale than to lose your money.

Moneymaker: If a customer wants to purchase a product, but doesn't have the money at the moment, offer to complete the sale as a layaway. Just take the cash the customer has available as a downpayment. Then hold the merchandise until the customer can return with the rest of the payment.

---

2. Avoiding Credit Card Fraud

When a business does choose to accept checks, odds are pretty good that it cashes the checks within a day or two. As a result, the business is pretty aware of which transactions are rejected and which are accepted. However, with credit cards, it can actually be more difficult to tell that a transaction has a problem. Typically, credit cards transfer money directly into your business bank account within a day or two of the sale. However, since credit card charges can be disputed by customers even after the business has received the money, some businesses don't even realize that a charge has been disputed! Since most of these disputes have a finite window to respond to the claim, these businesses can miss their window of opportunity to prove the charge was legitimate. As a result, the customer receives the money back.

How does this happen? It is actually very easy for a customer to get his or her money back from a credit card charge. All the customer has to do is to call the credit card company and say that the charge is not authorized and that he or she disputes the charge. Unfortunately, credit card companies do not require any proof that the charge is fraudulent from the customer. At that point the credit card company will send you a letter telling you the charge has been disputed and asking you to prove it's real. If you can't, the credit card company will reverse the charges and debit your account the full amount. This means that as a business owner, you will suddenly see money come out of your bank account as the credit card company takes the money back and returns it to the customer. To make matters worse, since many credit card holders don't check their charges frequently, the dispute can come weeks or even months after the original charge is made.

Now, you may say that customers who have had their credit card stolen have the right to get their money back. This is true. Unfortunately, the credit card company does not handle any of the costs of the fraud. The credit card company simply reverses the fraudulent transactions, since according to the credit card provider, it is your responsibility to ensure that the transactions are legitimate. As a matter of fact, if the credit card company finds that you accepted transactions that were not legitimate, it can actually cancel your merchant account for that type of credit card.

Unfortunately, this means that business owners have to decide which transactions they will allow and which they will deny. Many businesses make these decisions based on the risk of making the sale. If they can verify the purchaser, the sale is a lower risk. If they can't easily verify the purchaser, it may not be worth making the sale. When a customer is standing in front of you and you can verify the credit card signature or get a valid driver's license, this significantly lowers the risk that the business is opening itself up to a potential scam.

Taking credit card orders over the phone can be a bit trickier. If you can ship the product to the billing address, there is lower risk, but what about a customer that wants to make the purchase over the phone and have the product delivered to another address? Is it worth the risk?

One business had this experience. A new customer wanted to make a purchase for about $1,000. The sale included about $600 in merchandise, and about $400 in service for delivering and installing the product in his home. The customer was local to the area. The customer said he would be unable to pay the bill himself and asked to allow his mother to pay the bill on his behalf. To make it even more interesting, the customer was in one state, while his mother and her credit card were in another state. Immediately, the owner became concerned that this could be a potential scam. Although $1,000 may not be a lot to some businesses, to this business it was a significant sum. Therefore, this sale was given special attention.

Since the cardholder was in another state the business requested and required special validation before it would accept the credit card over the phone. To do this, the business called the credit card owner, looked her up online, and called the credit card company to verify the charge. Unfortunately, the credit card company wouldn't verify her authorization. The cardholder (i.e., the mother) called the credit card company herself, and had the credit card company then call the business to verify her identity. Of course, the business owner was still wary. After all, it wouldn't be too difficult to have a third person in the scam pretend to be from the credit card company. To ensure that the call really came from the credit card company, the business asked the credit card representative for her name and her call-back number. The business then looked up the number online, confirmed it was related to the credit card company, and then called it back to receive verification. Only after all this was completed did the business agree to do the transaction. Over the next month the customer called once or twice with warranty questions and discussed his purchase with the staff. The business was then satisfied that it had made a good sale.

You can imagine the owner's surprise when, two months later, the credit card company sent a letter notifying the business that the transaction was reversed because the credit card owner disputed the charges. To make matters worse, the business was also told that it would no longer be able to process transactions for that type of credit card because the credit card company claimed that the business participated in fraud. The business owner argued that the credit card company itself had confirmed the owner's identity and cited the name of the credit card representative. The credit card company now claimed it would never have verified proof of identity. The business was then told that accepting credit cards over the phone should never be done. Since the business had just spoken to the customer a few days earlier, it tried to contact him and discovered he had recently been convicted for fraud in another state. Next the business contacted the mother, and received no answer. The call went straight to voice mail. Without a solid paper trail including a signed credit card receipt, the business was unable to sway the credit card company to allow the charges or to reinstate their merchant account. It was devastating for the business.

In desperation, the business called the mother and left another message. This time the business detailed the situation it was now in and let her know that they would be forced to pursue her for fraud because she was the individual who had confirmed the credit card information. Fortunately, that message received a response. Eventually, the charges were corrected and the merchant account was reinstated.

 **Lifesaver:** Whenever you are dealing with any disputed charges make sure you keep track of who you spoke with recording the person's first and last name and get his or her direct number. Also, if you do send any original documents to a credit card company, make sure to save copies of each document as your evidence of responding to the claim in a timely manner.

It would be nice if there were foolproof ways to ensure that your customers would never be able to make fraudulent credit card charges, but, like checks, if you accept credit cards, you will run into credit card fraud. There are, however, ways to protect your business. The following are some simple rules that will both prevent customers from using fraudulent credit cards and ensure that if a transaction is disputed, you have the necessary paperwork to prove the claim:

- Always make your customer sign the receipt. Check the signature on the receipt against the signature on the back of the card. If the card is not signed, asked for photo identification. Note that some people do not sign their credit cards because they want this extra validation on purchases.

- Always keep the signed receipts. If you have any disputed charges, a signed receipt is one of the only ways to prove that the charge was legitimate. Keeping these items will save you money in the long run.

- Keep your customer information. If you track customer addresses, contact information, or other details, retain it for at least a year. This will ensure that you have any contact information you need to review, understand, and fight disputed charges.

- Avoid accepting credit cards on-site. If you do on-site or home delivery, get the customer to give you the credit card before you arrive at the location so that you can run the purchase through. This will ensure that the card is still good (i.e., has enough credit for the purchase and has not been reported stolen). If you cannot process the credit card before you arrive at the location, take the credit card on-site and call your office for someone to process the credit card for you.

- Ship products to the credit card billing address. If you are taking a credit card over the phone and shipping out product, try to ship your product to the credit card billing address. If the charge is disputed, providing the delivery receipt to the billing address may help to sway the credit card company that the product went to the actual customer. Taking credit cards over the phone and shipping to another destination leaves your business very little evidence to prove the charge was approved by an authorized cardholder.

- Check your credit card transactions daily. Before you even receive the letter in the mail saying that a transaction was disputed, chances are that the credit card company will already have reversed the transaction and taken the money out of your account. As soon as you see this reversal, call the company to get the information about what charge was rejected. The sooner you know about the bad charge, the sooner you can try to resolve it.

- Work directly with the customer. While most disputed transactions are disputed because of real fraud, in some cases customers believe that disputing a charge is another way to get back at a business that they had an issue with. Disgruntled customers will occasionally dispute perfectly legitimate claims in the hopes of getting even for some imagined problem. Although it is usually easy to work with the credit card company, send in the paperwork, and have the sale confirmed, you will still have an unhappy customer who is spreading negative information about your business. Therefore, you may want to call the customer and try to resolve the issue. If you choose to refund the charge, make sure that you do it as a refund. Under no circumstances should you ever be convinced to let a disputed charge stand if it was legitimate.

- Respond to disputed charges quickly. If you think a charge is being disputed incorrectly, make sure to respond quickly. Even if you are right, you only have a limited amount of time to reply. Don't lose your standing with the credit card company over a delayed response.

Moneymaker: Keep an eye on the fees charged by your merchant account. Depending on the credit cards accepted and how the credit card is run, the costs can change. The least expensive way to run a credit card is usually to swipe the card directly into a merchant machine and to post transactions every night. However, it is possible to incorrectly post transactions and incur fees of more than 5 percent. Therefore, make sure all your employees know how to run each credit card at the lowest cost possible.

---

3. Preventing Shrinkage and Outright Theft

Unfortunately, if you have a storefront, you will be considered a target for some type of criminal activity. Some businesses have the unfortunate experience of being held up at gunpoint, whereas others may experience nothing more dangerous than some small shoplifting. However, if you take precautions, it may be possible to reduce your risk of theft by making your business as difficult to rob as possible. After all, in many cases, would-be criminals will visit your store once or twice before actually completing a criminal activity. By reducing the attractiveness of your business as a target you effectively reduce the likelihood of a robbery.

What is most difficult about securing your business is that in order to protect your assets, you have to spend more money. Therefore, before you choose to implement any security measure you should always check the cost of the theft. On the one hand, if your business sells T-shirts that cost you $5 for 20, you probably don't have to worry about elaborate security systems. In this case, the cost of a high-end security system would exceed the cost of having one T-shirt stolen each day for a year! On the other hand, a high-end electronics store with plasma TVs could be significantly impacted with just one large theft. Even with insurance, the cost of the lost sales while the inventory is replaced, plus the cost of the new, higher insurance premiums would easily outweigh the costs of any security system that could be purchased.

Determine what your business is putting at risk and from there, decide your store policies. Accepting checks and credit cards, installing alarms and cameras: These decisions should all be made after their cost effectiveness is known. Further, these decisions need to be reviewed regularly. Businesses change over time and in some cases your security will also need to be scaled accordingly.

3.1 Reduce the payoff

Make sure that your business doesn't take in large sums of cash. If your business accepts credit cards, criminals may understand that your sales will not result in large quantities of cash. If your business requires cash only, then try to reduce the amount of cash available with a one-way safe or other device. Make sure to post a sign in your store that indicates that large amounts of cash are not present.

Even if you use a safe, make sure to remove cash from your store regularly. Frequent bank deposits will ensure that you don't lose a significant sum in case of a robbery.

Lifesaver: If you experience a break-in or robbery, make sure to file a police report. This can save you money in three ways. First, having this documentation can ensure that you aren't charged for a false alarm. Second, since you can write off any losses on your taxes, if you are ever audited, you may need documentation about the theft. Lastly, if you're lucky, the police may find your stolen goods.

3.2 Lock up valuables

If possible, make sure to keep any small valuable items securely stored. For example, jewelry stores take all valuables and lock them up at night, but this same principle can be applied to any business with small items that can be easily stolen. Safes are typically inexpensive compared with the cost of losing a large amount of valuable items.

3.3 Install a security system

If you don't already have one, adding a monitored security system may provide some additional security. Plus, as soon as a break-in occurs, the criminals will hear the alarm and know that police will be there soon. This immediate response may prevent thieves from getting as much as they could have without an alarm.

Installing security cameras can sometimes deter criminals because they don't want their image to be captured on film. Also, if you do have a robbery, having a security camera will allow you to prove your loss to your insurance company as well as provide an image of the criminals to the police.

If you can afford it, you may want to upgrade your security cameras to allow remote access. Being able to see your cameras from anywhere in the world allows you to immediately view your business if any problem or issue arises. This can make a difference when you security system goes off at 4 a.m. and you can immediately confirm for the police if there is a robbery in progress or just a false alarm.

3.4 Get steel roll-down doors

If your business has high priced items, it may be worth investing in roll-down doors. While many landlords will not allow these doors on the outside of a business (it may appear to make the neighborhood look more dangerous than it is), many, if not all, will allow you to place these doors on the inside of your business. In this case, they will be relatively unnoticeable, but criminals will not be able to easily break in — especially if you lock the doors with solid padlocks.

3.5 Work with your landlord and neighbors

If your area has regular break-ins, you may want to work with your landlord and business neighbors to get more attention to the problem. Community pressure may increase the number of police patrols or compel other deterrents that may reduce crime in your area.

3.6 Watch your customers

While there is a fine line between hovering and helping, it is important to make sure you are available to all your customers. The extra benefit is that if someone is planning on committing a crime, this type of assistance may deter the theft. Beware of "teams" though. Some criminals will pair up. While one individual is distracting an employee, the other will be committing the actual crime.

Lifesaver: If you do have a large theft, it may be beneficial to offer a reward for information leading to the arrest of the individual. Post a picture of the thief in your store, put the security video on YouTube, or take advantage of any other method you can to help solve the crime and get your merchandise back. Even if you do not receive your stolen goods back, this may be a low-cost way to deter the next theft.

4. What to Do If Your Employees Are Stealing

Unfortunately, many business owners experience theft not only from external sources but from internal sources as well. What is even more difficult is trying to determine if your employees are the ones causing inventories to shrink and cash to disappear. If you suspect employee theft, you can choose to eliminate the individual on the spot. However, you may have to pay unemployment and increased unemployment insurance if you fire an employee without documented cause (suspected cause is probably not enough). With these additional costs, it may actually be more expensive to fire a stealing employee than it is to wait until you can confirm the theft.

You may want to put the following measures into place to ensure your employees are not stealing money or inventory:

• Security cameras: For employees, security cameras can be a significant deterrent. Keep an eye on the cameras regularly and pay special attention to placement. If they are constantly being moved away from the register, or if the view of high-end items is being obstructed, you may have an internal problem. Even if you can't afford to hook up the cameras, just getting nonworking cameras installed may discourage your employees from taking the risk.

- Complete inventory reviews: When employees know you are keeping track of your inventory on a regular basis they may be less likely to steal as they know it will be noticed. Even if you can't do a full inventory, completing a regular inventory on big-ticket items can have a significant impact.

- Don't leave employees alone: If possible, try not to have only one employee in your store at time. (Obviously, this is not practical for all businesses).

- Ask trusted employees: What many business owners find is that some employees may not volunteer complaints about co-workers, but they may speak up if asked. Taking a moment to ask if any unethical behavior is occurring may get you more information than you expected.

5. How to Avoid Business Scams

Of course, not every business owner you encounter will be honest or even a real business owner. Sometimes it is difficult not to get taken in by a good sales pitch and a strong promise of success. However, investing in the wrong opportunity can be expensive. It can cost a business thousands of dollars, cause a loss of customers, and ruin a reputation. When these things happen, the tangible and intangible costs can be astronomical.

Some opportunities are lucrative propositions that will make millions in the long run, and others are not. There are numerous stories of people that invested in something at just the right time. Providing start-up capital for a small business or obtaining the first territory for a big selling product can result in windfalls in the millions. However, for every story of success, there are hundreds of stories of failures. Sometimes the business never existed in the first place, other times the owners squandered the funds received, and then there are always questionable products that were doomed for failure from the beginning. The question is how can you tell the diamonds from the frauds? When you are evaluating a new business venture, there are a few questions that you must always ask:

- How long has your company been in business? Don't just take the person's word for it. Check the company directories (e.g., Better Business Bureau) to confirm how long the company has existed. Beware of any "new" company that hasn't yet had a chance to incorporate. If a business owner is planning on growing, it is important he or she incorporates to protect the interests of the business.

- Have you ever had any problems with customers? Take the opportunity to research the company online to confirm the person's answer. Don't just check the business's website; do searches using the company name and other keywords such as "complaints," "problems," and "lawsuits." If anything comes up, find out what the underlying issue was.

- Do you have any references? Try to find other individuals that have had dealings with the company in the past. Ideally, try to choose companies you already know. If you don't know the business, research it. The business could be part of the scam. If the dealings didn't go well, find out why — remember, fault could lie on either end of a deal.

- Who are your competitors? Another sign of a scam is a business that is "so new" that there is "no competition in the marketplace." While a product can be unique, there is always competition. Before any new product is launched, a legitimate company will spend a tremendous amount of time researching the competition — this should be an easy question for the business to answer.

- Have you ever owned any other businesses? Some people are chronic crooks, so look up his or her business partner as well as his or her business. If a person has a history of defaulting on contracts and deals, chances are you will find the information on the Internet somewhere.

Lifesaver: To check on a business's credit rating, look them up on Dun & Bradstreet (D&B). D&B is considered the leading supplier of business credit reports worldwide. For less than $50, you can search a company's records including credit evaluation, lawsuits, liens, judgments, and bankruptcies. This relatively small cost can save thousands in dealing with companies with bad credit.

- What investment have you made in this product? A real company with real opportunities will typically have the financial backing of the owner as well as his or her close family and friends. If there is a "reason" why the person can't "take advantage of the opportunity" and is passing it on to you, you should beware.

- What problems have you had with your product? Almost any product or service has flaws; if it doesn't, it probably isn't real. A company that is creating a product will have already run into a few issues and should be prepared to discuss them.

- What are the contracted terms? Most legitimate businesses won't get into a partnership without an official contract. This is to protect them as much as to obligate you. If they are willing to work with you with no documentation in place, you are both unprotected.

- Do you have the patent on this? Unless the idea is already in the public domain or is a service, the company should be trying to patent a new invention. If the idea is truly valuable, the company should have taken steps to protect the idea.

WARNING:

Avoid any business deal that is cash-only. Requiring a money order, cashier's check, or hard dollars may be the sign of an illegitimate venture. While it is possible that it is a legitimate opportunity, it is nearly impossible to track your funds or get a refund from an illegitimate vendor. Paying by check or better yet, by credit card, will allow you more control of the transaction and ensure that you have a way of getting your money back if there is a problem.

- What is your product warranty? Most companies will warranty their products in some way. If you are purchasing a product, make sure that you get a copy of this warranty in writing.

- Can I have your company information so that my accountant, lawyer, and/or technical partners can look it over? If the company or person does not offer you documentation so that you can take time to review it, the opportunity is almost certainly a scam. No legitimate business will prevent a customer from "coming back tomorrow." While sales may be over or deals may change, no legitimate product will disappear in one day.

- How much should my company expect to earn? Most legitimate businesses will provide numerous disclaimers since earnings for any business venture vary based on the reseller or the economy. If a company starts making guarantees of "too good to be true" earnings, odds are it is not a real deal.

These questions are just a start. Before investing in any business venture you will need to do a significant amount of research. Many scams count on the "mark" being so interested in making money that he or she is willing to act quickly, out of greed. Therefore, take your time. Ask all the questions you want and be suspicious of the answers. As the saying goes, if something sounds too good to be true, it probably is. What you will find if you take this strategy is that many "great opportunities" quickly reveal themselves eventually to be the scams they are.

19

ENSURE THAT THE FUNCTIONS CRITICAL TO YOUR BUSINESS ARE STABLE, BACKED UP, AND INSURED

In any economy, businesses are fighting for survival and they just can't afford to waste time, which is a business's most precious asset. Let's say that overnight, all your computers have crashed and you have no email or any way to receive or send out orders. Consider how many days your business could survive if you didn't have any computers. If you can't find your customers' telephone numbers, or you can't do the payroll, or you can't pay your taxes, your business could be dead in the water unless you can get it back up and running right away. If many years' worth of critical information is just gone, what do you do now?

You can't let this happen. It's irresponsible to yourself, your employees, and your customers. You can't risk everything you've built because you wanted to cut a few corners.

It is imperative to add security that can protect your business's survival in case of large-scale problems. With the right technology solutions, and legal and financial products, it is possible to manage any business venture through any situation. Having these tools properly set up for your business can save your company money and time when a problem does occur. This can mean the difference between continuing to provide great customer service and failing to deliver on your company's promises.

If a business wants security for its data and company, these items are generally set up while the business has no issues. Spending the money and time to put these strategies in place is sometimes rejected by business owners as unnecessary expenses. Without the proper strategies in place when a problem occurs, it is impossible to recover quickly. After all, it is never possible to get insurance when you need it most — after a problem happens. The consequence of this decision can be far-reaching and devastating to a business. Many businesses lose money each year because they haven't invested in securing their business data, trademarks, copyrights, or management.

One business owner we know learned this lesson the hard way. The owner's business was heavily dependent on technology. All of his customer documents were on his main office computer and that computer was no longer working. When it was plugged in, it wouldn't even start. The diagnosis was bleak — the hard drive had been damaged and was no longer working. To make matters worse, the owner had never backed up these precious documents onto any other media. Without these documents, he could no longer complete any client orders. All of the work his business had done over the last two years was effectively lost. Data that could have been recovered if he had a backup plan in place was now inaccessible. His business was in jeopardy. Luckily we were able to recover the data and his business was able to complete its orders. However, the cost of recovering the data was much higher than it would have been to simply back up the data in the first place. He lost about two days of access to his computer, had to pay the cost of recovering the information, and had the stress of dealing with customers while the diagnosis was still unclear. With just a small investment in backup media, he could have avoided the entire incident. Needless to say, today, his business's data is much more secure.

WARNING:

Backing up a computer completely means you save your application software as well as your data. Many times, files cannot be opened if the original application that created the file is not available. To save applications, it is easiest to make copies of the original software CDs. Don't forget to document the key if necessary. An easy way to do this is to simply write the key on the CD with a permanent marker.

1. Easy, Low-Cost Data Backup

Almost all businesses today use a computer to track some part of the process. It may be their point-of-sale system, accounting system, customer information, or any other function. In general, if your business maintains any data on a computer, your should be backing it up and storing it at a safe location. If you don't have the data properly stored, you are at risk for a variety of accidents. Technology failure, such as the hard drive problem described in the example above, is actually the most recoverable. When hardware fails, there are sometimes ways to recover the data although they may be very expensive.

Recovering data due to malicious activity can be much harder. Disgruntled employees can delete data, remove files, and damage your machines in ways that make it hard to notice the problem as soon as it occurs. By the time it comes to light, it may be too late to recover. Another common way to lose data is when a business computer becomes infected with a malicious virus or spyware. While most people know to avoid questionable sites, there are times when even the most innocuous sites can cause damage. For example, a young woman we know was simply checking her local church website while on her lunch break at work — nothing could have been more innocent. When she tried to access a file she found that her computer wasn't working properly with the site. Instead of calling anyone, she just tried another computer. By the time she realized there was a problem, she had accidentally downloaded a virus that destroyed the data on both computers!

What can be done to protect your information? The cost of implementing a backup procedure will depend dramatically on the amount of data your business has, how often it needs to be backed up, and what type of recovery you want to have. There are many ways to back up your technology — everything from simple solutions such as copying files to CDs or DVDs, to more complex solutions such as storing data off-site with an outside vendor.

In order to determine which backup solution is best for your business, you should always contact a professional who can help you find the most cost-effective solution. Technology is constantly changing and improving. Although it may cost a few dollars to get a professional opinion, the advice a professional can provide will be well worth it.

1.1 Media backups

Media backup means copying critical data from your computer onto transportable data such as CDs or DVDs. This is one of the least expensive and easiest ways to back up your computer since most computers are equipped with either a CD or DVD writer. The only investment for most companies is the cost of the CDs or DVDs.

This method is relatively simple. Creating backup CDs or DVDs is very similar to moving data from one folder to another. Most computer users can learn this skill quickly. If you choose to back up files in this way, you should try to create backups at least once a week and retain at least one copy per month so that you can always restore your old files.

Once you have the CDs or DVDs created, storing the disks off-site (e.g., at your home or in a bank vault) provides additional security in case of fire or theft. One downside with this method is that users have to remember to regularly copy the data and take it off-site. Some owners or employees may not regularly complete this function and data can be lost.

1.2 Computer hard drive arrays

If your business cannot afford to wait for your data to be recovered, or if your data changes moment-to-moment, there are technology solutions that will help keep your data accessible. One such possibility is to create an array (collection) of hard drives on your computer. In this situation, the computer stores data onto all the hard drives in such a way so that even if one hard drive breaks, the data is still available. This type of redundancy can be costly; however, it requires no human involvement once it is up and running. The limitations of this method are that the data is still in one place. If your business has a flood or fire, the computer will be ruined and the array will be useless.

1.3 Off-site backups

You can use an outside vendor to copy data from your computer to an off-site location. This method requires an Internet connection and it is generally recommended that computers are left on overnight for backups to occur. If there is a need to recover information, you can then copy the data back onto your computer from the company website. Off-site backups are one of the most secure, reliable ways to back up your computer.

The cost can vary depending on which vendor is used and what type of Internet connection is required. Setting up the backup may be difficult for some users, but once this is regularly scheduled, it requires little employee intervention. Backups are generally completed automatically with most companies providing nightly backups. Since the storage is completed by an outside vendor, off-site, there is no need to store any data.

Once again there are limitations to this method; since the data is stored off-site it is only accessed through the Web. If you don't have Internet access, your data is not accessible. Also, if you need to recover an entire machine, it may take a few days to download all the necessary files.

Moneymaker: Maintaining complete records for all of your client and customer purchases can become a revenue source. Some companies and individuals may find themselves in a position in which they would like a copy of all their old records. Having this data available will allow you to run these reports for a reasonable fee.

---

2. The Risks Associated with Saving Information Longer Than Necessary

Most business owners are aware that some data always has to be saved. Signed credit card receipts are considered necessary if you ever need to debate a customer charge. Vendor bills may be required if you are ever audited and need to provide evidence of your business deductions. Company incorporation documents and employment records may need to be kept almost indefinitely.

Most business owners and managers are aware that there are laws that require them to keep information about their business for some minimum amount of time. As a result, to keep things simple, many owners default to simply saving all their records as long as they can. What many don't realize is that keeping data longer than the required periods can actually pose a risk to the business. If there is a lawsuit or inquiry, it is possible for all data regarding the matter to be included in the investigation. Even if the law only requires you to retain information for seven years, if you have data going back ten years, this data can now be included in the investigation. Thus, if a problem is found, your business can now be accountable for not only what happened in the last seven years, but for what occurred before those dates.

3. Uninterruptible Power Supplies (UPS)

Almost every business today uses some sort of computer technology to manage the company. From a simple home-office computer to large business servers, most companies will invest in computer technology at some time. The cost of this investment can be anywhere from a few hundred dollars to tens of thousands of dollars for one machine. Whatever size your business, the technology investment needs to be protected.

Some business owners believe they will save money by avoiding the costs and expense of protecting their technology. However, power fluctuations, both too high and too low can wreak havoc on computer systems. Many people buy surge protectors because they are aware of the damage that large bursts of electricity can do to computers. What many people don't realize is that this is not the only risk. If your power is not properly regulated, it can fluctuate and damage a computer just as badly. That is where an Uninterruptible Power Supply (UPS) with Automatic Voltage Regulation (AVR) comes in. This device actually regulates the amount of electricity that connected devices receive. In the case of a blackout, the UPS also acts as a battery, allowing the technology connected to run a short time longer (maybe 30 minutes or so) so that the system can be powered down safely.

4. Insure Your Business Assets

If you have a mortgage, you are required by your broker to have homeowner's insurance. If you drive a car, you are required by the government to get car insurance. The reason why both of these requirements are in place is because it is commonly accepted that accidents can be costly, and even the most careful homeowners or drivers may find themselves at fault in a lawsuit. The costs of an accident could run the individuals thousands and sometimes hundreds of thousands of dollars. However, there is no such requirement in some places that all businesses must have insurance. This means if you are sued, the entire settlement would have to be paid by your business! If your business is small, you may find it preferable to simply declare bankruptcy and fold than to try to pay. Owners of larger businesses may lose everything and find themselves starting over. Purchasing insurance before any incident occurs could save your business from the difficulties and risks of a lawsuit later on.

As your business grows, you may find your coverage needs to be changed as well. The same way your homeowner policy needs be reviewed and updated when the value of your home changes is the same way your company insurance policy should be reviewed and updated when your business changes. Adding more employees, company vehicles, or locations should all be preceded by a call to your insurance agent to see if your insurance will cover the new situation. If it does not, inquire as to what insurance is available for your company. Although it may seem costly, the best and only time to buy insurance is when you don't need it.

WARNING:

Keep an eye on your own personal insurance. As you start insuring your business, you may find that some of your coverage is now redundant or may no longer be valid. For instance, if you own a rental property in your name, your homeowner insurance may allow you to cover it. However, if you transfer the property to a new business entity, the new "owner" must also be a named insured on the policy or it may no longer be in force.

5. Patents, Copyrights, and Trademarks

Almost all businesses try to build and market a brand or product. When a business does grow large enough to be truly successful, it will find many imitators that try to infringe on the brand marketing and product line. The best way to protect a business from this sort of theft is to patent, copyright, and trademark any intellectual capital as you go. Although it is possible to fight lawsuits like these without actually having these legal items in place, it will be significantly easier for your business if you do.

6. Get Rid of Piles of Paper

If your business is very paper intensive, you may find it difficult to manage all of that documentation. Some businesses can find themselves drowning in paper. They often have a hard time finding documents they need, have an unruly amount of filing to complete, and often pay high costs for off-site storage when the files are closed.

However, for many businesses, especially for doctors and other medical professionals, each piece of paper is important data that is required for proper treatment. One local medical imaging office found a great solution to this predicament. Instead of simply handling boxes and boxes of paper, they scan all of their customer information electronically. When a customer walks into the office, he or she is asked to fill in the standard medical forms. After the customer completes all the appropriate forms, the office assistant sits down with the individual to review the paperwork. The office assistant electronically scans the form into her computer system through a small scanner that sits on her desk. As she reviews the paperwork, she also confirms the customer's information in her system. Everything from a scan of the customer's insurance card to the full medical history is then entered directly into the computer. By the time she has finished her five- to ten-minute interview, she has completely set up the patient profile and has "filed" all the paperwork. Two weeks later, the original paper documents are destroyed and all that remains are the electronic copies. Of course, this business has regularly backed-up computer systems since the data is not backed by any paper files. The solution is relatively easy to implement and just requires a few good scanners and a reasonable electronic filing method.

Lifesaver: Before you consider storing boxes of paper off-site, look into scanning these documents into an electronic format instead. Sometimes the cost of maintaining off-site storage can be expensive, especially if you need the paper files retained for the next few years. It may actually be more cost-effective to hire a scanning company rather than a storage company!

7. Make Sure You Have a Backup Plan for Your Job

One of the most critical parts of any business is often its owner. This individual sometimes has more abilities and rights than anyone else in the organization. He or she can sign checks, has authority over utilities, has signed for lines of credit, and is sometimes irreplaceable. If this describes your situation, your business may be at risk. When a business owner has too much authority and no backups, the company can easily fail if the owner fails to be able to work even for a short time. Although it is sad, many businesses have had to close their doors when something unexpected happened to the dedicated, hardworking owner. While the family may try to maintain the business, without proper instructions and authority, it may be next to impossible.

The best way to protect your business is to ensure that it is properly set up while you are well. As with any other situation, if you wait until a problem occurs, it will generally be too late. When families are worried about a loved one, they often don't consider the financial impact until it is too late. To get this done right, your legal counsel will need to create a plan that is most appropriate for your business.

Consulting with your accountant will also help ensure that nothing has been missed. There are actually many options to ensure the security of your business and to give your family the best chance to continue to keep your business alive.

In our case, we set up a family trust that clearly outlines how the business is to be handled if something were to happen to us. Another step we take is that at least two people are listed on all business accounts when possible. Although this may seem like a morbid project, the value to your family, should they need it, will make it worthwhile.

8. Test Your Backup Systems

Even with all proper backup procedures in place, you cannot be sure that your backup system will work as designed when you need it. There are too many businesses, both large and small, that have only realized their backup tapes were blank when they went to restore a broken system. The only way to ensure that your systems are in place and working properly is to completely test your backup functions.

For technology, the test is simple. Check all of your backup media regularly to ensure you have the files you need to recover your critical systems. For a more thorough test, take these files to a new computer and try to load and run everything you need.

To test the backup of your resource team, you only have to allow each employee to take a vacation and make it your policy not to contact the employees while they are out of the office. If your systems are properly functioning, everything should continue running well, no matter who is not in the office. If you find that any function breaks down, this is a task that needs a better backup put in place.

The last and most critical test is to make sure that your business can continue to run without you, the business owner! If you want to be confident that your business will survive an illness or absence, it is best to test these functions before a problem occurs. You should be confident that your business will be able to run smoothly, and even prosper without you to guide its day-to-day activities. After you believe you have the correct team in place to make this happen, you need to be able to test them. It is not enough to have the team be able to get along most of the time without you. The current management team needs to survive without you for extended periods if you want the business to survive your absence.

To test the team, take a week out of the office and stay out of contact. Do not answer the phone, return a text, or send an email. Just take a vacation, get out of town, or start exploring your next business opportunity. When you return, spend two days still "out of touch"; in other words, don't answer questions. During this time, audit what has happened in the previous week. Check sale records, talk with regular customers, and get feedback from management and employees. The first time you do this, you may find that there are many issues that need to be resolved when you return. Customer service quality may have dropped or problems may not have been resolved correctly. This is to be expected. Continue to work with the team to retrain them in these areas until you believe that they are ready. Repeat the process and leave the business for another week.

What you may find is that it will take longer than you expect to be able to walk out of your business and be confident that you have a smoothly running operation. This is not surprising. It will take time to get the team so efficient that they can run without you. Not that you may want to leave. Many business owners never get to the point where they choose to leave their first business. Others build their fortunes by creating processes and teams that survive for decades without the owner's intervention. Whichever business owner you want to be, your business will be more valuable and more profitable if your team runs as well with you as without you. Further, you will have more freedom and opportunity to enjoy your success if you are confident that your business is capable of growing on its own.

20
NOW THAT YOU KNOW THE "WAYS," CONTINUE TO SEARCH FOR NEW OPPORTUNITIES

We hope we've helped you take a new look at your business and that you're making absurd amounts of money. You've tightened down on your spending and your employees are happy and hardworking. Money is coming in, sales are through the roof, customers are building statues to you in the town square, you may even have taken a day off! So what's your next step? How do you grow even larger?

Well, once your business is successful, you may find that there is a limit to how far one office or storefront can grow, for many different reasons. A business location can only handle so many customers. Eventually, if you want to continue to grow your company, you will need to start exploring new options and new opportunities.

1. Expand Beyond Your Boundaries

While some businesses may be able to grow indefinitely from one office (e.g., web-based companies) others will have difficulties getting much larger while staying in one location. If your business has been growing quickly and then the growth slows down, it may be that you have saturated your immediate area. One way to tell if this is the case is by mapping your current customers. Applications such as Microsoft's MapPoint allow you to import all of your customers' names and addresses and then view this list distributed across a local map. What you may find is that most of your customers are from the immediate 10- to 20-mile area. In this case, you may need a second location to continue to grow.

Of course, if you are not a retail business, a full-blown second location may not be necessary. It is possible to expand into other areas through lower-cost options such as satellite offices or even remote employees. Depending on what your business offers and how the products and services are delivered, you may find that you can expand your market with much lower overhead than the costs of a full business.

2. Acquire Another Company

If you decide you want to expand, some companies find it easiest to expand by purchasing additional companies. Depending on what you are looking to do, you may purchase a business that is doing well and will immediately increase your holdings, or you may purchase a small company that does not have the right processes in place and can be redesigned to become profitable.

Expanding through purchasing has both benefits and risks. On the one hand, you are purchasing a fully functioning company that you can inspect and review. On the other hand, you now have to redesign the company to be consistent with your own business. Either way, it is important to review the profitability of another business and make sure you pay only what the business is worth. If chosen correctly, acquiring another company can be a fast way to expand with a more manageable risk.

3. Franchise Your Processes

Some businesses have such thorough processes in place that they may want to consider franchising. However, this can be more difficult than some business owners realize. The first time a franchise is tried, the business will need to invest tens of thousands of dollars in legal fees to set it up properly. After that, the company may find that supporting a franchisee is a separate type of business all together. More than a few owners that have tried this have had the franchisees eventually disassociate themselves and dissolve the contracts. We know one retailer that tried to franchise and they invested almost $50,000 in legal fees, created process and training documents, and sold two franchises after being in business for only two years. However, they were not prepared to support these companies. Within a year, both companies had taken legal action and had dissolved the relationship. Further, both companies were struggling to survive and were unable to match the original store's success.

However, there are obviously many franchises that have been started successfully and profitably. The key is to make sure that you are properly prepared before you take this path. Make sure that you have a mentor or advisor that can advise you on the best practices in this area. Taking the time to invest in learning this new business model can mean exceptional profits once done correctly.

4. Increase Your Holdings through Commercial Real Estate

For some companies, investments are another way to increase the company profitability without assuming much risk. One of the most popular ways to do this, especially in a slow real estate market, is to purchase a retail space that has enough room for your company as well as a few open locations available for rent.

When choosing a property you should be certain that the location will have cash flow (i.e., make money) as soon as you purchase it. This does not mean that the rental income from the property simply covers the mortgage. All expenses on the building or land investment should be paid by either your company's rent or the rent of all the tenants (including your business). Expenses include the mortgage principle and interest, taxes, insurance, property management, repairs, improvements, legal fees, accounting, and any other expenses you will need to incur to manage the property.

Too often, investors purchase real estate that loses money for years before any money is ever made. This puts an unnecessary pressure on the business to subsidize a poor investment. However, if chosen correctly, a real estate investment can actually save the business money as well as be a profit center:

- Constant rent: Like purchasing your home, if you get a fixed mortgage, the rent will be constant. Thus, as a business owner, it guarantees that you will not have to deal with increasing rental expenses each year (except for maintenance and improvements).

- Income source: If you purchase a location that has other rental units, you can make money as a landlord. If you don't want to spend your time managing and finding tenants, a property management company can easily provide these services at a fee.

- Appreciation: When you purchase any real estate, whether it is land or a building, you have the opportunity for that investment to appreciate. Over the years, this can result in unexpected dividends when you finally choose to sell the property.

When you are considering purchasing a property, always contact your accountant and lawyer. It may be that they will recommend setting up a new corporate entity to own the new property or may have a different structure in mind that will help reduce your tax bill and secure your investment. As with any large purchase, the structure you use to make the purchase can have long-term tax and legal implications so you should always take advantage of professional advice to make the best deal possible.

5. Take Advantage of New Opportunities

As a successful entrepreneur you may find that there are opportunities that are open to you that you haven't had before. You may find individuals presenting new business investments, real estate deals, and new product launches that you never would have known about just a few years earlier. When you have successfully run a small business for a few years, you can be certain that you are in an elite group of successful entrepreneurs. Many businesses are started each year and many close their doors that same year. If you have taken the time to grow a company and you have become profitable, you have learned more about running a business, facing the challenges, and overcoming the odds than most people will ever know.

Some of the opportunities presented to you may be profitable and others may fail. To choose which investments to pursue and which to ignore, you have to look at your own abilities. Consider what you enjoy most and what you excel at and put those skills together to find new opportunities. Don't be afraid to take calculated risks and pursue new areas of interest. After all, once you have successfully proven that you can grow a business, even through a tough economy, you are certainly ready for new challenges!

Feel free to visit www.19waystosurvive.com for more small-business resources you may need on your journey.